Organizational Traps

Organizational Traps
Leadership, Culture,
Organizational Design

By

Chris Argyris

Harvard University, Monitor GLP

OXFORD
UNIVERSITY PRESS

OXFORD
UNIVERSITY PRESS

Great Clarendon Street, Oxford OX2 6DP

Oxford University Press is a department of the University of Oxford.
It furthers the University's objective of excellence in research, scholarship,
and education by publishing worldwide in

Oxford New York

Auckland Cape Town Dar es Salaam Hong Kong Karachi
Kuala Lumpur Madrid Melbourne Mexico City Nairobi
New Delhi Shanghai Taipei Toronto

With offices in

Argentina Austria Brazil Chile Czech Republic France Greece
Guatemala Hungary Italy Japan Poland Portugal Singapore
South Korea Switzerland Thailand Turkey Ukraine Vietnam

Oxford is a registered trade mark of Oxford University Press
in the UK and in certain other countries

Published in the United States
by Oxford University Press Inc., New York

First published 2010
First published in paperback 2012

British Library Cataloguing in Publication Data
Data available

Library of Congress Cataloging in Publication Data
Data available

Typeset by SPI Publisher Services, Pondicherry, India
Printed in Great Britain
on acid-free paper by
MPG Books, Bodmin and King's Lynn

ISBN 978-0-19-958616-5
ISBN 978-0-19-963964-9 (pbk.)

1 3 5 7 9 10 8 6 4 2

To my Monitor colleagues
especially Mark Fuller, Chairman and CEO

Contents

Contents

Part II. How Conventional Approaches Bypass Traps—and What to Do About it

Introduction

What do Traps and their Consequences Look Like?

Anyone who has spent time in an organization knows that dysfunctional behavior abounds. Conflict is frequently avoided or pushed underground rather than dealt with openly. On the other hand, the same arguments often burst out again and again, almost verbatim. Turf battles continue for extended periods without resolution. People nod their heads in agreement in meetings, and then rush out of the room to voice complaints to sympathetic ears in private. Worst of all, when people are asked if things will ever change, they throw up their hands in despair. They feel like victims trapped in an asylum.

No one likes these aspects of organizational life, yet we feel powerless to change them. We want to change, but can't. We are stuck, trapped in the status quo. We've all heard comments like these:

You just can't talk to them honestly—they immediately get defensive.

They just don't understand.

Bob never listens—if you want to get anything done, you've got to go around him.

She ran the meeting as if it would be a group decision, but really she had already made up her mind.

Of course I couldn't say that to his face.

Nothing will ever change.

People express thoughts like these when they feel trapped. And people often *are* trapped. But they are not trapped by some oppressive regime or organizational structure that has been imposed on them. They are not victims. In fact, people themselves are responsible for making the status quo so resistant to change. We are trapped by our own behavior.

Although we say we value openness, honesty, integrity, respect, and caring, we act in ways that undercut these values. For example, rather than being open and honest, we say one thing in public and another in private—and pretend that this is the rational thing to do. We then deny we are doing this and cover up our denial. And in doing all this we trap ourselves.

Such accusations may seem astounding, but as I will show in the first few chapters of this book, this kind of behavior is commonplace and easily documented. We are trapped by behavior patterns that exist at all levels of organizations. We create Traps when the problems to be solved are likely to be upsetting and threatening to all concerned. These Traps inhibit effective problem solving and inhibit the detection and correction of errors. Traps are anti-learning and anti-corrective of the very errors they create. Traps facilitate blaming others for creating and maintaining Traps.

In short, Traps inhibit learning when learning is especially needed. These counterproductive consequences are found in all organizations, private or public, large or small, successful or in failure. They exist regardless of the gender, race, education, and wealth of its participants. I believe reducing Traps represents the next big challenge to raising the level of performance by individuals, groups, organizations, and societies.

Traps impair even successful organizations. As we will see in Chapter 2, even a very successful and innovative organization such as Intel can get caught up in behavior that traps it, strangling decision-making and causing conflicts that can grind things to a halt.

Traps Can Lead to Disaster

Not only are Traps anti-learning, they can yield unfortunate, even tragic, consequences. Consider these examples:

- Teachers help students to cheat on tests in order to get better funding. Teachers cover up their help.

- The 'best and the brightest' fail to see the problems they are creating. Indeed, it took Secretary of Defense Robert McNamara decades to admit that he and others were blind to the problems they created in their pursuit of the Vietnam War.

- The *Challenger* report, written by individuals at the top of their professions, promised that such disasters would not occur again. Several years later we had the *Columbia* disaster that occurred even though everyone knew and followed the recommendations and the report.

And as I write this part of the Introduction the financial world has built a series of multi-layered Traps that seriously threatens the economies of many nations.

In all these cases, policies, rules, and structures were in place to prevent such tragedies. These did help but they were not enough. Why? Individuals learn to protect themselves if caught creating or going along with Traps. For example, they blame others or the system. They deny any possible personal responsibility. Next they deny that they are denying by making the subject undiscussable. In order for that strategy to work they must make the undiscussability undiscussable. As a result of the above strategies, the individuals build a mind-set that they are victims of the system. They are helpless.

But in reality we are not helpless. The good news is that these powerful Traps can begin to be changed and reduced during relatively straightforward interventions that emphasize social and cognitive skills. Those who are committed to learning can develop the skills in the same amount of time that it takes them to learn to play a middling game of tennis or golf.

The Organization of This Book

The primary objective of this book is to examine the advice of thought leaders writing about organizations and their management. I have selected three topics, namely, leadership, culture, and organization design, because they are crucial in creating Traps and because they are crucial in changing them.

In order to achieve this objective it is necessary to present the theory and methods that I use to explain and to reduce Traps. Thus I begin the book with the presentation of new cases taken from real life in governmental and private organizations. The first case describes how Dean Rusk, the then Secretary of State, attempted to reduce the Traps that made the State Department so ineffective that it was called affectionately 'Foggy Bottom'. Rusk was genuinely committed to making the management of the department more open, transparent, and trusting. As we shall see, he managed the change processes in ways that strengthened the Traps that he sought to reduce. I chose this case even though it is old because my present informants tell me that, fifty years later, the analysis of the Traps still holds.

The second case is an updated version that Donald Schön and I presented about thirty years ago (Argyris and Schön 1996). Andrew Grove, the then CEO of Intel, advocated a more direct and candid aggressive form of hard power. Although Rusk was an advocate of soft power and the leaders used different leadership styles, the results did not differ. Soft power and hard power strengthened the Traps in their respective organizations. As we shall see, leadership style is not the crucial factor for reducing Traps. The crucial factors are what I describe as the theory of action that each leader uses (the theory-in-use) and the reasoning processes they use to make sense of the world in which they are leading.

In Chapter 3, I present examples from other organizations as well as educational programs to illustrate this claim. The theories-in-use and reasoning processes are the same in all cases. All the participants used what I describe as Model I theory-in-use and defensive reasoning. I expand the perspective by showing that if Model II and productive reasoning were used, it could begin to reduce the Traps and overcome the negative consequences.

In Chapters 4, 5, and 6, I present the advice of some of the best and brightest scholars and practitioners on leadership, culture, and organizational design. The advice they present, for the most part, is flawed. The analysis shows that, with one or perhaps two exceptions, the advice is not adequate to reduce Traps. Indeed, in most cases, the authors do not present advice on how to do this. In a few cases where the advisers imply that their advice can be used to reduce Traps, I present evidence that they actually strengthen Traps and appear skillfully unaware of the gaps and inconsistencies.

There is a tacit strategy embedded in the reviews of Chapters 4, 5, and 6 that I should like to make more explicit. The review of the literature is structured by the Theory of Action of myself and Donald Schön. The gaps and inconsistencies that I describe are derivable from our theory.

There are two implications. First, the review can be used to 'test' the features of our theory. For example, we should find that the gaps and inconsistencies occur under the conditions that our theory predicts. If Model I and defensive reasoning are primary causal factors of Traps, we should not find that the latter are caused by other factors, especially those that are contradictory to those that we specify. Second, if such hypotheses are not disconfirmed then it is possible to predict that the advice will continue to be flawed even though those who produce the advice agree that Traps are counterproductive to effective action. In effect the review can be used to predict that the flawed features of the advice will persist.

I should like to thank Dianne Argyris, Michael Beer, Philip McArthur, Robert Putnam, and Diana Smith for their helpful advice on early versions of the book. Lorraine Hines was a committed assistant and editor who saved me from difficulties that I created. Librarian Mark Blumberg provided me with a continuous flow of new books that our library had acquired.

Part I

Why We Act Against Our Own Stated Interests

1

How We Deal with Difficult Situations

As I noted in the Introduction, we say we value openness, honesty, integrity, respect, and caring. But we act in ways that undercut these values—not just once in a while, on very rare occasions, but regularly and routinely—whenever we face threatening or otherwise difficult situations. We then deny we are doing this and cover up our denial, thus trapping ourselves. In this chapter I will document how this works by presenting two examples.

I should like to introduce the reader to how typical behavior traps people by providing an extended example of how people at the State Department behaved in the course of a new initiative put forth by Dean Rusk, Secretary of State, who believed in and espoused genuine participation, the sharing of power with his immediate reports, and the creation of a culture that would encourage transparency and trust. As it turned out, this initiative was threatening to the people involved—and so led to the type of behavior I just described.

The Department of State and Secretary Rusk

President Johnson had asked Dean Rusk to make whatever changes he thought were appropriate in order to transform the State Department's reputation of 'Foggy Bottom'. Rusk and his immediate reports conducted inquiries to identify the sources for the negative reputation. They included the lack of openness, transparency, and trust. He decided to begin the changes at the top. He scheduled a meeting composed of mostly senior State Department officials and a few equally high-ranking officials from the Defense Department. To help with this meeting, Secretary Rusk asked me to be prepared to present the view of the senior ambassadors with whom I had been working to examine ways to create more openness, transparency, and trust at the highest level of the State Department (see below).

Rusk began the meeting with a genuine plea for change in individual behavior and the culture of the department. He then introduced an assistant secretary of defense who was the architect of the 'programming, planning, and budgeting' system of management. Secretary McNamara had used this concept to make the Defense Department more efficient and effective. Rusk assured those in attendance that if they thought these ideas were relevant to the State Department, he would champion their plan with a great deal of energy and enthusiasm.

After the presentation was finished, the Secretary asked for comments. There was silence. Secretary Rusk then asked me to respond. I predicted that the State Department officials would resist implementing such a program because they would see it as threatening to their careers (I describe these concerns in more detail below). Secretary Rusk again asked others to give their reviews. Silence. Rusk then asked one of our country's most senior ambassadors to respond, especially about the concerns that I had mentioned. The ambassador thought for a moment and then he said, in effect, Mr Secretary, if you and the President ask us to implement this new program, we will do so. After the session ended the ambassador came to me and said, in effect, that he actually agreed with me and he would say that to the Secretary at a meeting later. I asked why he did not say so during the meeting. He replied doing so would be inappropriate.

The next day the Secretary told me that he was surprised that the ambassador did not speak up during the meeting. After all, he had selected him to attend because he thought the ambassador would be candid and honest. I asked the Secretary if he had said that to the ambassador. The Secretary responded, no, it would have been inappropriate.

Rusk did not act consistently with the values that he was espousing such as openness, transparency, and trust. He selected the ambassador for candor and honesty, but did not tell him so—nor did he express his disappointment with the ambassador. The ambassadors, who agreed that these changes were of value and important, also did not act consistently with the 'new values' during the session. At the time of Rusk's initiative, I was working, as I noted, with a dozen of the most senior foreign services officers (assistant secretaries of state, and top ambassadors including several career ministers). I found much evidence that these men believed that a culture existed that required them to cover up when dealing with issues that could be upsetting and embarrassing to them or to the State Department. For example, tape recordings of their own private sessions (Argyris 1968) indicate that they thought *being open and transparent would be a recipe for organizational suicide*:

A. If I were to be very honest, I think that one reason I have succeeded is that I have learned *not* to be open; *not* to be candid. Suggesting that we should strive to be more open? That's like asking us to commit organizational suicide.

B. I agree with A. I have experienced situations where I sensed the superior was not leveling. I figured that he was trying to set up either a situation which would predispose me to his point of view, or he was trying to set up a situation where only one conclusion was possible.

C. And what did you say?

B. Not a darn thing—I let him continue.

F. Over the years, I developed a lot of evidence that my superior wasn't really leveling. It got so bad that one day I seriously thought of resigning. But, I didn't have the courage. I didn't ever tell him this.

B. Why not?

F. It would upset him.

The ambassadors during their own seminars said that they believed the objective was laudatory, but that it was naïve and would generate conflict and reinforce mistrust. In their view, talking openly and making the norms transparent would be 'career threatening'. Thus, the participants believed that the openness, transparency, and trust that the Secretary was requesting, would be seen as counterproductive by the community. They also believed that expressing their views would be inappropriate. By keeping silent, they covered over this conflict.

The ambassadors and assistant secretaries of state acknowledged that their distancing from the problem would reinforce the difficulties. They also acknowledged that this made effective change less likely. They reported that they were in a double bind. If they acted to implement the new program, they would be participating in career 'suicide' as well as opening up the State Department to massive internal problems. If the President realized the cover-up and undiscussability, it would prove to him and to others outside the State Department that Foggy Bottom was unchangeable. They also reported that they learned to live with the double bind by denying they were experiencing it and denying that they were denying.

Under these conditions much important dialogue goes underground. As a result a powerful circular loop is created—a Trap. It takes the form of a process within the Foreign Service culture that tends to coerce the participants to minimize interpersonal threat by minimizing risk-taking, being open, and being forthright, as well as minimizing their feelings of responsibility and their willingness to confront conflict openly. This, in turn, tends to reinforce those who have decided to withdraw, play it safe, not make waves, and to do both in their behavior and their writing. Under these conditions people soon learn that survival requires that they 'check with everyone' and make sure to develop policies that upset no one. And these actions and strategies are seen as rational responses to a difficult situation. Those involved are certainly not responsible for the situation, but its victims. And they are helpless to change things.

Traps are Universal

The State Department meeting was begun with a genuine plea by the Secretary for an increasing degree of openness, transparency, and trust to champion the entire effort. On the surface the discussion was rational, thoughtful, and diplomatic. Traps were activated by what was occurring below the surface. For example, Rusk was concerned about resistance. He developed tactics to strengthen his position (e.g. by the invitation of the senior ambassadors and myself stating my doubts). He did not mention his feelings and fears or these tactics. He acted as if he was not making his concerns undiscussable and their undiscussability undiscussable although he was doing that.

The ambassadors and senior officials also had concerns and doubts. For example, a genuine implementation of the policy being espoused would violate organizational cultural norms as well as placing their careers in jeopardy.

They made these issues undiscussable and their undiscussability undiscussable and acted as if they were not doing so. So much for openness, transparency, and trust.

But surely, the reader may protest, the State Department is a unique organization; this sort of behavior must be very unusual. But my research indicates otherwise: in fact it is nearly universal. My colleagues and I have studied the behavior of well over 10,000 individuals, of both sexes. They include individuals with varying degrees of education and wealth, people who work in private and public organizations or as independent practitioners. When facing difficult or potentially embarrassing situations, most of them acted in ways that created Traps and most were skillfully unaware that this was the case.

We have visited many organizations whose leaders told us that they practiced openness and honesty and that organizational defensive routines were notable by their absence. So far, we have found neither claim to be true.

We diagnose individuals' theories in use by asking them to write cases (as explained in Chapter 2), by observing their responses to our cases, by observing and tape-recording the participants in action, and by listening to tape recordings they made when we were not present. The fact that we get similar results when we use different diagnostic methods, and in a variety of different contexts, strengthens our belief that people get trapped in the same patterns of behavior whenever they experience threatening or embarrassing situations.

As we will see, people get trapped by using patterns of behavior to protect themselves against threats to their self-esteem and confidence and to protect groups, inter-groups, and organizations to which they belong against fundamental, disruptive change. As human beings become skillful in using this pattern of reasoning, they develop a defensive reasoning mind-set that they use to explain their actions and to design and implement future actions. This happens in all sorts of organizations. Let's look at a fast-paced high technology company—far different from the venerable State Department.

Intel Corporation

The second example is Andrew Grove's leadership actions during his tenure as Intel's CEO. Grove believed that it was important to hire bright individuals who knew the technology and science that are relevant to their tasks. They should have a lot of energy to work hard and be dedicated to the governing values of Intel. The individuals should have the courage of their convictions. They should do what is right, not what they are ordered to do.

Grove describes his leadership as managing individuals' performance by focusing on the important details. He rewards individuals' performance by using strict, quantitative procedures that are credible and transparent. The focus should be on content and not style (Argyris 2004; Grove 1996). His strategy for effective leadership includes the following:

1. Advocate your position clearly in the service of winning the argument. Sell and persuade. Be detail-driven and expect clear-cut choices. Nothing mushy like, 'it seems that' and 'perhaps'.

2. If individuals get into an argument, listen in order to surface any inconsistencies and gaps. Point them out and expect the participants to resolve them or 'I will'. Strive to synthesize the views into a coherent whole.

3. Advocate your views in ways that minimize exposing your own inconsistencies. If inconsistencies are surfaced by others, explain them by saying, in effect, I am forced to this because of others' actions.

4. 'Vectorize' which means establish a direction, a point of application, that is filled with energy and commitment.

5. Strive to educate others who appear to disagree. If education does not work, then romance those who are not cooperative and who delay progress.

6. Be demanding but fair. Subject all claims to test. Exclude discussions of leadership styles because such discussions are highly subjective and difficult to test.

Grove's subordinates interpret his use of 'hard power' as containing the following reasoning.

1. I know what I want them to do.

2. I will tell them directly and openly.

3. I will expect them to understand.

4. If they do not understand, I expect them to say so.

5. If they say that they do not understand I will repeat, explain, and clarify my position.

6. If they disagree, I will expect them to try to argue me out and I will do the same. The basis for winning is rigorous reasoning and not personal style.

7. If they do not comply, I will (*a*) give them more time to think 'constructively', (*b*) argue with them, and (*c*) find ways to stop the discussion until I generate new ideas to sell my position.

The dilemma that the subordinates face is that this reasoning is part of Grove's leadership style. Yet, he maintains that leadership style is not relevant and should not be discussable. The subordinates have developed their own strategies to deal with their dilemma. For example:

1. Sense Grove's mood.

2. If he is confused he gets tough. He bulldozes everything in his way. He tells anyone who is in his way to get lost—to get out of the way.

3. Once he has made up his mind, it is difficult to change it. If he does change his mind, he often does it without acknowledging it.

4. Remember, Grove is unaware of his actions. Or, if he becomes aware, he is likely to blame others.

5. Keep these rules in mind when you craft conversations with him. Do so by acting as if you are not using these rules.

Effects of Unilateral Leadership

Grove's acts in his unilateral leadership pattern are intricately involved with the way he discusses the substantive issues. As he behaves consistently with his belief that discussing style should be out of bounds, he also increases the frustration of his subordinates. They, in turn, deal with their frustration by developing strategies as to how to deal with Grove. The subordinates' reasoning for doing so is that Grove has outlawed discussion of such matters. The subordinates, in turn, cover up their strategies and cover up this cover-up. All the players espouse openness and transparency yet they act in ways that inhibit both features and they cover up doing so.

Grove (1996: 90) describes the dynamics during discussions when the ideas about the right direction of the company split people. When the stakes are high, there will be a growing ferocity, determination, and seriousness. 'People will dig in. These divergent views will be held equally strongly, almost like religious tenets. In a workplace that used to function collegially and constructively, holy wars will erupt, putting coworkers against coworkers.' Teamwork, motivating employees, became harder, almost impossible Grove reflected on the interactions, 'I was talking to people who didn't want to hear me. As I got more and more frustrated that people didn't want to hear what I couldn't get myself to say, I grew more blunt and more specific in my language.' 'So we debated endlessly' (p. 90) and played weird games of trying to trap each other. They were trying to make a decision between two different and strongly held beliefs. 'Rational discussion was practically impossible' (p. 91).

In the case of Intel, Grove openly espoused transparency and trust. He espoused that these features could be created by individuals who were rigorous thinkers and had the courage of their convictions. He activated the creation of Traps by espousing that effective personal leadership styles were irrelevant. If some believed that leadership styles were relevant, he openly insisted that their views were wrong. Indeed, he excluded discussions about interpersonal impact.

The subordinates believed that Grove's leadership style was inhibiting openness, transparency, and trust even in technical and business issues. They activated Traps by defining rules that would minimize their frustrations as well as endanger their career.

Thus Grove champions openness, transparency, and trust in technical and business issues. He outlaws the discussion of interpersonal styles. Grove is consistently open on his position. He crafts rules that make it dangerous for the subordinates to express their feelings and views. The subordinates adapt by creating their own 'survival rules'. They too make their rules undiscussable in public. They also drive the undiscussability underground and act as if they do not.

The Perniciousness of Traps

These examples and the others spread throughout this book show that, almost uniformly, we deal with difficult situations by *not* dealing with them. We find ways to pretend to engage and in fact manage to avoid engaging and keep what we are doing hidden from ourselves. At the State Department, the top personnel gave lip service to the new program, but did nothing. Secretary Rusk didn't follow up or challenge people to live up to their words promising action. At Intel, when the stakes were high and decisions urgent, teamwork ground to a halt. People dug in and decisions didn't get made.

The participants in both cases acted in ways that activated Traps. They said that they did so not to embarrass or make others defensive. The intention was to show respect and concern for others.

In both cases the Trap behavior became self-reinforcing and self-sealing. Behavior is *self-fueling* or self-reinforcing in that the actions taken reinforce the defenses that caused the problems in the first place. For example, behavior that leads to covering up problems leads to more cover-ups—and sometimes ever more elaborate cover-ups to guard against the cover-ups being exposed. In other words, when we cover up, that fact itself must be covered up. The cover-up process is self-fueling. (Lying is also self-fueling: 'Oh what tangled webs we weave when first we practice to deceive.')

Behavior is *self-sealing* when it only permits behavior that accords with pre-existing assumptions. At the State Department, high officials kept silent, explicitly refusing to test whether openness and honesty could improve things. Thus, the view that honesty would be career suicide was sealed off from rational exploration. At Intel, Grove wouldn't permit discussions of leadership style, thus sealing off his belief that style was irrelevant from any sort of challenge or criticism.

In both cases the participants denied personal responsibility for their actions. They acted as they did because of the behavioral system that was out of their control. They were victims, they were helpless. Traps can last for many years even if attempts are made to reduce them. They will appear unchangeable until the participants decide enough is enough.

The processes to *begin* to reduce Traps will become activated if the participants focus on their personal responsibility in creating the Traps and examine the validity of their claim that they are helpless victims. Genuine change will begin only if the participants come to see the validity of the insight asserted by a sage: we saw the enemy and it is us.

Should the reader still feel the cases discussed here are exceptional, in the next chapter I will present more detailed examples of the sort of behavior that creates Traps, showing how ubiquitous it truly is.

2
Actions that Trap us

Let us now look in close detail at how people behave in ways that entrap them, by presenting cases in which people, using their own words, describe their actions in confronting a problem and what they were thinking and feeling at the time. No doubt, readers will recognize situations that resemble ones they themselves have experienced. In fact, the patterns of behavior shown in this chapter are so ubiquitous every reader should recognize himself or herself in one or more of the cases.

Comparing a person's public actions with his or her private thoughts can be quite revealing. The method that we have used to do this is quite straightforward, and is called the left-hand–right-hand case method.

The Left-Hand–Right-Hand Case Method

We have developed a relatively simple case method that is easy to implement and not time-consuming. The case method makes it easy to describe the behaviors used by someone during an encounter with another person. The case method does not require that the description be a perfect recollection.

This case method has been used effectively (by a conservative guess) with over 10,000 individuals representing varying degrees of categories such as gender, race, age (12 years above), education, wealth, roles in organizations (of all types), from the lowest to the highest levels (where 'all types' includes governmental, voluntary, families, communities, religious groups) during the past three decades. The case is relatively easy to complete: it usually requires about a half hour.

The case method asks the individuals to describe an incident that he or she believes is important to improve his or her effectiveness and the organizations' effectiveness. The individuals are asked to reflect on any thoughts and feelings they had while producing what they said and did not express openly. This helps to identify self-censoring processes that are being used. They help to complete pictures of what is going on when the individuals are planning their actions and then carrying them out.

Below I present the actual instructions used to explain to people how to write a left-hand–right-hand case.

Directions for Completing the Left-Hand–Right-Hand Case

First, in a sentence or two identify a problem that you believe is crucial and that you would like to solve in more productive ways than you have hitherto been able to produce.

Second, assume that you are free to interact with the individuals involved in the problem in ways that you believe are necessary if progress is to be made. What would you say or do with the individuals involved in ways that you believe would begin to lead to progress. Write a paragraph or two.

Third, assume that such an opportunity did arise. How did you act? Or, if the situation has not yet arisen, describe how you would act.

Fourth, divide your paper into two columns. In the right hand column write what you said (or would say if the session is in the future). Write the conversation in the form of a play. For example, you might begin by saying, 'Thanks for taking the time. This is an important meeting for me (and I believe) the organization.'

Next, write how the other person (or persons) responded. It too should be in the form of what they actually said. For example, 'It is always a pleasure to get together with you to solve important problems.' Again, if the meeting has yet to occur write what you think they might say. Do not worry about whether your recollections or predictions are perfectly correct. The key criteria are that you believe that what you have written is close to what you recollect happened or what you predict is likely to happen.

In the left-hand column write whatever feelings and thoughts you had while you were speaking that you did not express. You do not have to explain why you did not make the feelings and thoughts public. Continue writing the case for about two double-spaced pages (or more if you wish). When you finish, read the case to make sure that you wish to base your learning on what you have written. Next, if you are doing the exercise alone, place it in a drawer and return to it in a few days. The same directions apply if you are conducting this experiment with several others.

There are two purposes for using the case method to be described. The first is to understand, explain, and connect your actions with the effective implementation of your intended consequences. The second purpose is to show how the case method can be used to test empirically the predictions that you make.

After you have finished the discussion of your case with the others, we will examine what was said and done in order to assess the validity and generalizability of what you wrote before the session, and how you acted during and after the session(s).

A Preliminary View of the Cases

Case 1 shows how a dialogue between a superior and a subordinate is dominated by defensive reasoning that results in focusing on an issue that is highly technical. On the surface, the two parties argue about technical details, but the superior's left-hand column shows that the superior's concerns really have little to do with the technical aspects of the case.

In Case 2 I describe how it is possible to use the case method to help individuals realize, in a relatively large group and with limited time, that they actually inhibited the learning that they were trying to create. Moreover they realized how unaware they were that they were creating the negative consequences.

Case 3 was used in class where there was time to discuss the cases in more detail because the members were assigned to smaller groups. Philip wrote a case that depicts how he advocated a position against Steve, evaluating Steve's actions negatively, and making attributions about Steve's intention. The case ends badly for Philip, but he does not reflect on how he himself contributed to the negative outcome or what he might have done differently. The presentation ends with suggestions as to how Philip could have made his dialogue more effective.

Case 4 illustrates one of the most common strategies we have found that people use when they have to talk about negative issues such as evaluating poor performance. They ease in. When delivering negative evaluations, people ease in and justify doing so in the name of concern and caring, cover up their true feelings, and act as if they are not doing so.

Case 5 illustrates how a diagnosis can be made of the interactions between a CEO, a CIO, and the latter's subordinates. The conversation was hot and the IT professionals failed to convince the CEO of their position.

The case ends with examples of the sort of actions and productive reasoning that might have helped.

Case 6 shows how a class of advanced MBA students advocated for their position without offering evidence. Rather than offering evidence, they simply emphasized their personal conviction that their position was correct and refused to budge.

Case 1: Submerging the Primary Issue

A superior (S) wrote a case about his relationship with a subordinate (O) regarding the latter's inadequate performance around certain information management systems. The case illustrates that S's doubt about O's performance is driven by S's belief that O avoids taking responsibility to solve the technical problems. First, let us describe the case that S submitted before he arrived at the seminar (see Table 2.1).

In reading the right-hand column, the dialogue appears to be about the delays around the compiler and debugger. The performance of both machines and their interaction is specifiable in technical terms, namely, in terms related to the domain of computer and information technology. Indeed, the disagreement between S and O, as it appears in the right-hand column, is crafted primarily in terms of technical issues.

Let us now expand our view. S wrote that he was frustrated with O's performance. S doubted O's explanation for delay, namely, that the debugger could not be tested

Table 2.1. S's case

Thoughts and feelings	Actual conversation
I am concerned (angry) about what is a continual problem.	S: We need to find ways to have your group deliver part of the product on time.
	O: It is simple. We cannot test our de-bugger until the compiler has finished all its testing.
I sense that he is avoiding responsibility for the problem.	S: Are there any tests that can be run before the compiler is ready?
My feeling is that the group should accept responsibility.	O: There are limited tests that can be run but the cause of the most difficulties is in the compiler/debugger interaction.
	S: But is it possible to capture correct compiler output and run your tests against that?
I again see the avoidance. I want to lead him toward a solution where he can take responsibility.	O: Sure, we could do that, but it would not catch where the compiler has changed. Besides it would also take more disk space. It is simple: we are dependent on the compiler.
I feel that he cannot concede the point and will move to other issues as an escape.	S: First of all, disks are cheap. If you need more space, we can get it. Second there are other components that interact with the compiler that do not have the same problems with delivering.
I begin to feel frustration. I'm canceling out the additional excuses.	O: The other components do not interact as closely. Look at the last release. The compiler added new features, and we did not find out until the end.
I am led in another direction.	

until the compiler finished testing. This claim could have been tested because the technical theories involved specify the performance features of each machine and their interrelationships. But this technical test was not requested or required by S.

One reason that S did not force such a test was that he believed that the important issue was that O and his group were avoiding their responsibility. S was faced with a leadership and group-performance issue. This claim is illustrated by the left-hand column comments. Yet the case suggests that S acted in ways that suppressed the primacy of the interpersonal–organizational defensive issues. He appeared to hope that by making the technical issues primary he could, through appropriate questioning, eventually surface the leadership and group-performance issues. S's strategy was, therefore, to make secondary what he believed was primary and to cover up that he was using such a strategy.

O, on the other hand, crafted his conversation to deal with the technical issues. He was able to distance himself from the interpersonal–organizational dimension that upset S. This resulted in a counterproductive dialogue. S began by noting that disks were cheap (technical). If S provided more space (technical), and since other components interact with the compiler (technical), then the technical problems could be resolved. O found reasons why S's technically based solution was inadequate. S saw O's emphasis on technical issues as further evidence that O was acting irresponsibly. O could argue that he was doing so because he had not been told of S's view of O's irresponsibility.

The case illustrates that S acted in ways that drove the human problems underground (left-hand column) in order to minimize making O defensive. S covered up his real concerns by focusing only on the technical issues, and never engaged O about his unhappiness over O's avoiding responsibility. O, in his responses, remained at the technical level and appeared to be designedly sidestepping and acting as if this were not the case.

Each individual in crafting his arguments focuses exclusively on technical issues (compiler/debugger interaction) and states them forthrightly. Each has little choice but to be forthright in this respect, because it is hard to distort technical features based on publicly documented information without giving the other party the opportunity to falsify the claim.

Thus, S also crafted his conversation in ways that cover up his feelings and acts as if he is not doing so. The difficulty with this strategy is that it makes it easy for O to remain at the technical level and sidestep issues of personal responsibility.

We have a conversation, therefore, that is unlikely to resolve the problem that S believes is crucial (O's avoiding responsibility). If O is sidestepping because he believes that S's requests are unfair then that problem will also not be solved. S and O can end the conversation by privately attributing negative evaluations to the other party, each feeling that he is dealing with a difficult individual.

What result from such a conversation are the self-fulfilling prophecies that are characteristic of Traps. Indeed, as we will see, this sort of behavior is endemic to Traps.

Case 2: Closed to Learning

This case is based on a seminar I held with a group of financial executives. The focus of the seminar was on new concepts of procedures used in strategic cost management and on the human problems likely to arise when such concepts and procedures are implemented in organizational settings.

We were not able to discuss all the cases the financial executives wrote because there was not enough time during the week-long seminar. At the outset, the faculty member used the full set of cases as a vehicle to provide the entire group with an overall picture of the underlying action strategies they used. Three lists were developed. List 1 contained examples of comments quoted verbatim from the 'left-hand columns'.

List 1

1. Don't let these guys upset you.
2. Say something positive.
3. This is not going well. Wrap it up and wait for another chance.
4. Remain calm. Stick to the facts.
5. He is clearly defensive.
6. He's playing hardball because he is afraid of losing power.

7. She is over blowing the systems issue to avoid having to change.
8. He is baiting me now.
9. Will he ever be able to change.
10. This guy is unbelievable. He will never change.
11. You are nowhere as good as you think you are.
12. The trouble with you is that you do not really understand accounting as a managerial function.

The classroom session began with the executives (all of whom had written cases) reading List 1. After a few minutes, the faculty member asked them to describe their reactions to the list. He asked, 'What does this list tell you about the individuals who wrote the comments? What inferences do you make as to what is going on?'

The executives responded easily and quickly. Eight examples of their comments, taken from the transcript, were as follows (List 2).

List 2

1. They were opinionated.
2. They talk as if they are right.
3. They are frustrated and angry.
4. They are entrenched.
5. They are avoiding conflict.
6. They are not listening.
7. They are fearful.
8. They exhibit lack of empathy.

The faculty member wrote these responses on the board. He then asked the participants to reflect on the nature of these comments. The executives responded that their responses indicated an overall negative reaction. The comments were primarily negative evaluations ('They were opinionated/entrenched') and attributions of defenses in others ('They are avoiding conflict/not listening'). Moreover, the class comments indicated that the executives thought the writers of List 1 (whom they knew to be themselves) appeared closed to learning.

The faculty member helped the executives to identify the following general patterns.

- Evaluations and attributions are made in ways that do not encourage testing. The writers appear to act as if their diagnosis is valid and does not require testing.

- The writers appear closed to learning or, at least, they see learning as unnecessary. Yet all of them attended the seminar and wrote the case with the expressed purpose of learning how to be more effective in dealing with the human side of enterprise.

The class comments on List 1 led to reflection on a different issue. One executive said that what surprised her was the negativeness of the first list. She recognized her comment in List 1 and it, too, was negative. Yet, she added, she was certain that her intent was to be positive. She was unaware of the discrepancy and unable to say how she created it (skilled unawareness and skilled incompetence).

The faculty member then asked the executives to analyze List 2, their comments about List 1, as he had written them on the board. The executives responded that these comments too were negative. They were evaluations and attributions crafted in ways that did not encourage inquiry. This also surprised them.

Here we find another predictable pattern:

- There appears to be systematic discrepancy between the writers' expressed aspirations to learn and help others to learn and their actual behavior, which is largely counterproductive for learning.
- Individuals are systematically unaware of the ways in which they produce their unawareness.

The faculty member then said that the dialogue so far illustrated some of the main findings that had been obtained worldwide from nearly (at that time) 6,000 individuals of both sexes, ranging widely in majority or minority status, education, wealth, and organizational rank. What the class participants were experiencing was not unique. It seems that individuals throughout the world deal with difficult, embarrassing, and threatening issues in a similar manner. For example, they make evaluations and attributions that are crafted in ways that do not encourage learning. They are predisposed to be unaware of the discrepancies they produce, such as aspiring to be positive yet being negative.

Case 3: Competing Models

In presenting this case, I quote heavily from Martin's book, *The Opposable Mind* (2007). The author of the case is an MBA student identified as Philip. He writes:

Immediately after graduating with my undergraduate degree I started up a small internet company with two friends who were in similar situations. The time of the following encounter was a little over one year after we started the company. We had done well, in the sense that the company made enough money for us all to live on. However, we all felt as though the company had stagnated over the past few months, that our initial momentum to 'be wildly successful' had given way to running the company merely to meet our lifestyle needs, which were very modest.

We attributed this stagnation to the fact that we hadn't formally divided up ownership of the company. It was registered as sole proprietorship in the name of Steve, one of the three of us. With the company being his sole personal liability, he was unwilling to take the kinds of risky/big moves that Keith and I were interested in taking to grow the company. Conversely, while Keith and I had worked very hard initially to build a foundation for the company, we were now unwilling to 'give our all' to the company, bringing it to the next level, before we knew that we were going to have an equal stake in any success we might help create.

The purpose of the encounter was to establish the ownership percentages of the company so that we could go forward with it.

What I Wanted to Accomplish and How I Hoped to Do So

I recognized that Steve was a phenomenally talented guy who took the initial step to found the company, and as a result he could be 'first among equals' once ownership shares were formally established. However, I saw the company essentially as a venture of equals and I wanted the ownership shares to reflect this—say, 40/30/30 for Steve, Keith and I (or at least something very close to this).

I hoped to achieve this outcome by explaining my reasoning and viewpoint along these lines. I thought that skills and time commitment to date of all three of us was prima facie evidence that we all essentially were equals, and that unless we codified this the company couldn't move forward.

Table 2.2 outlines the way the meeting went.

Within a month after this meeting [Philip continued], I had accepted a job in a large IT company. Steve and Keith continued the internet consulting business. Keith left about a year after I did. Steve shut down the business three years later when he went to business school for an MBA. In all that time the business didn't 'grow' in the sense that we originally discussed, though ultimately Steve made a good living from it, alone, before going back to school.

My concern is this: while I don't generally expect anything from people other than self-interest, is there any way that I could have approached this situation to have 'helped' the other people involved to appreciate that my position was probably the course of 'enlightened self-interest?' After all, while Steve 'won' (or at least kept) 100% control, 100% of not much is still not much. What could I do in the face of this way of thinking? Or am I thinking about this all wrong even now?

It is easy to see how Philip could come away from the original interaction reinforced in his antipathy toward clash; reinforced in the belief that there is little hope for constructive resolution in the face of clashing models. According to Philip, Steve 'won' and he asked plaintively and largely rhetorically: 'what could I do in the face of this way of thinking?'

Table 2.2. Philip's case

What I thought and felt but did not say	What we actually said and did
	Me: I guess the fundamental questions we have to address is which model of equity division are we going to approach: one where there is a distinct difference between one of us versus the other two, or one where we're all generally equal, but with variations that reflect different skills or other contributions.
Steve, yes you're talented, but get a hold of yourself—you're not that much more talented. Besides, I'm the one who held this company together while you finished your last year of school.	Steve: I feel as though my contributions to date warrant a fundamentally different level of control from the two of you. Also, as it stands right now, I have 100% control over the company. Why on earth would I move myself from the current situation, where I have control, to one where I don't? What if the two of you decide to gang up on me?
	Me: As far as your observation regarding relative contribution to date goes, I disagree. I think we've all given a hell of a lot to the company, with no one of us head and shoulders above the others. Regarding your observation about giving up control, put yourself in our shoes—that is the situation that Keith and I are in right now, only worse! It only takes one of you to 'gang up' on the two of us.
You always have felt as though you're some kind of 'special case' haven't you? I knew you were a control freak, but now I'm beginning to see how much of one you are.	Steve: I am unmoved by your arguments. Since I'm the boss currently, my own opinion regarding worthiness wins. And whatever reasons you and Keith had for accepting the current situation are your own, and I don't feel as though they apply to me.

Table 2.2. (*Continued*)

What I thought and felt but did not say	What we actually said and did
	Me: While I can't speak for Keith, I can say that the reason why I've been willing for you to be 100% to date has been that up until now, it really hasn't been an issue of much practical importance. We're on the cusp of growing the company, taking on much more risk and hopefully getting much more reward than has been the case in the past. If there's big reward to be had, I want my share. But I think the fundamental issue is what is going to happen next for this company. I feel my talents are needed for this company to move to the next level, and I don't plan on giving them away without getting a level of equity acceptable to me as a result.
Steve, you moron! Do you really think that? Is this just a negotiation ploy, or has your ego detached you that much from reality?	Steve: I disagree—I think this company can grow without the kind of equity division that you describe, one where I lose control.
Keith, you moron! Don't you realize that I am fighting for you too?	Keith: I think it is clear now that Steve isn't going to move from his position. That's OK with me. If that's the way he wants to play it, then that's the way it will be.
Oh I get it. You're just being a weasel because you're worried about paying your rent next month. You got no balls!	
	Me: With this outcome, I don't believe that this company has a long-term future, and so I have to look for my own best interest to see if something else out there is going to work out better for me.

Martin answers: try something other than pure advocacy in the face of an opposing model. We help the participants notice that, other than a pair of rhetorical questions by Steve (Why on earth would I move myself from the current situation, where I have control, to one where I don't? What if the two of you decide to gang up on me?), neither Philip nor Steve inquires into the perspective of the other. Each repeatedly advocates the merits of his own model and shows little or no interest in the logic of the opposing model. Even Keith advocates (implicitly) that Steve is wrong: but that since Steve isn't going to change his position, Keith is OK with it.

Both Philip and Steve focus on advocating their own points of view. Each goes to lengths to advocate his model vigorously and thoroughly. Both see their primary task as explaining enough of their model so that the other can understand it and thereby accept it. When the accepting part doesn't seem to happen, each advocates more forcefully or refutes what they understand to be the other's model. They signal to one another that each is completely uninterested in the other's model.

The participants also become progressively angrier. From Philip's comments in his 'left-side' commentary, we see him going from seeing Steve as a 'talent' to being a 'control freak' to being a 'moron' in the space of several minutes. The anger seeps over to the 'right side' in more inflammatory language ('I don't plan on giving them away') and more extreme positions ('so I have to look to my own best interests'). Advocacy fuels the responses that fuel the anger which fuels more advocacy and more anger and so on.

Neither learns much about the other model and particularly the thinking behind the model through the advocacy of each. Without significant learning about the other model, it is very difficult for either party to come up with a creative resolution. A creative resolution requires more features to become salient and/or more/different causal relationships to become apparent. A creative resolution requires assertive inquiry. The conversation could have gone much differently if, after Philip's first advocacy, Steve had responded with 'I understand that you feel that your share of economic return of the business is too low. I was curious whether you had given any thought to the issue of managerial control? Do you also feel that you have too little managerial control or is your issue primarily in economic stake?' Or if after Steve's existing first advocacy, Philip had responded: 'I understand that managerial control is important to you. I have two questions. First, are you agreeing that my stake in the economic return is too low or am I misinterpreting you? And second, could you tell me more about your concerns about sharing control with Keith and me?' Both responses combine an advocacy—one that is based on a restatement of the other's point—with an inquiry—an assertive inquiry into the details and thinking behind the opposing model.

This alternative inquiry produces several valuable side-effects. First, it opens up a cornucopia of new salient data and causality regarding the opposing model that can be mined for creative resolutions. Second, it convinces the other person that you genuinely care about the views that produced their model, even though it opposes yours. And third, this tends to cause the other person to inquire into your model, which gives them ideas on creative resolution as well.

And frankly, in this case, the creative resolution isn't far from the surface. Philip focuses on increasing his economic payoff and Steve focuses on not losing managerial control. These concepts actually aren't particularly in fundamental opposition. A dual-class share structure with Steve maintaining 51 percent voting control and Philip gaining a substantial economic interest (with disproportionately less voting control) would seem a relatively straightforward resolution if both weren't so focused on the logic of their own model.

Case 4: Easing In

One of the most frequent strategies individuals use when they are trying to tell the other of her or his inadequate performance is to ease in. I should like to illustrate an easing in case by borrowing heavily from one written by Manzoni and Barsoux (2002). The boss in this case used an easing in strategy to avoid making the other individual defensive.

In an attempt to avoid the threat associated with such head-on, possibly escalating, confrontations, many bosses choose ease in to approach the interaction less forcefully. Rather than stating upfront their unilateral evaluation of the other's problem, they try to finesse the issue by leading the subordinates to reach the 'right' conclusion alone.

This tactic, called 'easing in', was chosen by an executive who had a difficult piece of news to communicate to one of his subordinates.

The strategy of easing in allows the principal actor to demonstrate concern and caring. He and all others who ease in create a situation where caring and concern means covering up one's true views and acting as if he or she is not doing so. Not surprisingly, the other also covers up his true feelings and acts as if he is not doing so. The result is ineffective learning and the taking of responsibility away from the employee.

Framing by the boss

Here is how the boss presented the situation:

As chairman of the company's committee for product development, I had to ask one of the members to leave the committee, as she did not contribute satisfactorily to the committee's work. In her daily job this manager reports to me, so we talk often. She performs very well in her daily job as manager of a small group, so the reason for poor performance on the committee could easily be too much work. I do not think she will like this conversation as the conclusion will be that she must leave the committee and lose status, which is of greater importance to her than many other people.

Easing in is a risky strategy. The first risk of easing in is that it relies on the subordinate to be willing to provide the 'right answers'. If he fails to do so, it may be difficult to rescue the conversation before the relationship gets

Table 2.3. The boss's case

Thoughts and feelings	Dialogue
I will make her feel that her daily job is important and that she is too busy to participate in the committee.	Boss: Are all deadlines met? And how are you and your group?
	Sub: We have met all deadlines except one, which was caused by a break-down in our equipment. It is not easy but I think that we are all working very hard, and I must admit that I am very tired in the evening when I go home.
I will make her see her role in the product development committee.	Boss: Do you feel that you are sometimes wasting time when we have product development committee meetings?
	Sub: Yes. Sometimes I cannot see the connection between the points being discussed and my part in it.
I must make her understand that she is doing OK in respect to her daily job, but that she does not contribute to the group process in the product development committee.	Boss: I also feel that you sometimes are a bit absent-minded and do not get involved in the process. Maybe because your thoughts are with your daily job.
	Sub: Yes, that is true.
Now is time to launch the bad news, when she has just acknowledged the small size of her own contribution.	
I do not want her to push back on this, so I will not ask for alternative solutions. I will present the one solution that I want.	Boss: Could it be of benefit to you and the group if you were no longer a permanent member of the committee, but were invited when your expertise was required?
	Sub: Yes, that could be a solution if at the same time I get a copy of the agenda and the minutes from the meeting.
She must not lose too much status or enthusiasm in her daily job, so I will let her have the copies.	Boss: of course, you will get the copies.

damaged. In this case (see Table 2.3) assume for example that the subordinate answers the boss's second question ('do you feel that you are sometimes wasting time when we have meetings of the product development committee?') by saying, 'No, I think these are great meetings and I love to watch you chair them; I learn a lot.' The second risk is that a boss who eases in and pretends not to do so is essentially covering up. The boss is representing herself as open-minded but in fact has already made up her mind. The problem is that we have all sat in front of bosses who tried to ease us into a decision they had already made, and we generally found out somewhere along the way that we are not in a real 'discussion'. And if we didn't find out on the spot, we found out later. In most cases, we understood that the boss was being disingenuous with us.

If subordinates catch their boss being insincere, they are likely to spend more time asking themselves what else the boss is keeping up her sleeve. At the very least, they will not get a sense of self-determination and relatedness from the interaction. Their boss is treating them like a pawn, leaving them the alternative of playing along or resisting and provoking a confrontation. Our view is that, other things being equal, easing in is a bad idea for a boss, especially if you know ahead of time that you are almost certain to get caught!

Overall, the boss framed the issue narrowly: 'Let's get her off the committee with minimum breakage.' This framing almost dictated the choice of tactic: 'This is going to be pretty tricky, so I'd better control the discussion pretty tightly.' The boss could instead have framed the interaction loosely: 'I have this great subordinate who doesn't say much on the committee, her career plans, and how committee membership fits in them.' This framing would have been much less threatening for the boss and would not have required a unilateral approach designed to maintain control over the interaction and 'win'.

Case 5: The CIO and the IT Group

The chief information officer (CIO) of a large electronics firm was told by the CEO, his superior, that an important organizational problem existed and had to be corrected. The problem was that the Information Technology (IT) group was too large and too expensive. Moreover, its service to the line organization was inadequate.

The CEO reminded the CIO that this was not the first time he had spoken of this problem. He was becoming impatient. He warned that if costs did not go down and if the quality and efficiency of service did not become better, he would be forced to take drastic action that could include finding a new CIO. The CIO called a meeting of his immediate reports to take corrective action.

CIO and his immediate reports

The CIO opened by telling his subordinates that he had received a 'read-our-lips' order from line management: cooperation was non-existent, and the information professionals were providing minimal value added, despite higher budgets. He then said, 'I want to discuss with you our ability to react to users' needs and the facts that we are always having difficulties with line management. They are, after all, our customers. We must be concerned about meeting their needs.' The information professionals responded as follows:

- We are concerned about their needs. The big trouble is that they do not know what they want.

- When they do (know what they want), they have no idea how long it will take to provide them with high-quality services. They want everything yesterday.

- We have 'had it up to here' with line management's complaints. The problem would be easily solved if the line gave us the people and resources we truly need.

The CIO expressed empathy with their frustration and anger and he suggested that they might begin to turn things around by developing 'a credible plan to respond to (customer) needs'. The professionals responded in the following way:

- There is no sense in planning; our users don't plan. Anyway, we are convinced that just about the time we think we are on top of things, they will make more demands and complain about what we are failing to do.

The CIO replied:

But since we do not have a solid plan, we cannot review the way we are managing our resources...As I see it, we have two choices. The first is to do what we are doing—and I believe that will be disastrous. The second is to break out of this mold and change the way we do business.

Members of the group countered by arguing that there was no way to change line management. As one said, 'If you want to try, good luck.' The CIO replied, 'If planning isn't the way to go, how do you propose to solve the problem?'

The direct reports responded with increasing emotion. They said in effect,

1. The problem is not solvable because line management makes impossible requests.
2. The information professionals are already killing themselves.

'That's why the good people are leaving', said one individual. 'I agree', said another, adding, 'It is not fixable.' Virtually at the end of his patience, the CIO explained: 'We have to fix it because we have no choice! Otherwise we are not responsible.'

What is going on here? Clearly the information technology professionals are expressing frustration with and mistrust of the line executives, as well as their own superior. Their conversation is crafted in a way that makes a dialogue difficult. For example, they advocate their positions and make evaluations and attributions about line management in ways that do not encourage inquiry or testing. These are examples of their unillustrated, untestable evaluations and attributions about line management:

- Line does not know what they want.
- Line makes demands with unrealistic deadlines.
- If we meet their demands, they will follow up with more unrealistic demands.

- The problems are unfixable because of line management's recalcitrance.

The CIO's reaction

The CIO wanted to get the subordinates to be cooperative, and he also wanted to minimize the likelihood that they would see him as unfair and judgmental. Unlike his subordinates, he censored his evaluations and attributions and acted as if this were not the case. Asked to write out his private thoughts and feelings, he offered the following:

- These guys act like a bunch of babies.
- They do not realize how insensitive and opinionated they are.
- Sometimes I feel that I should read the riot act to them. They've got to wise up or all of us will lose.

When asked what led him not to make these thoughts and feelings public, he looked astonished, 'If I said these feelings and thoughts, all I would have done was add fuel to the fire.' He was correct. His private thoughts and feelings were crafted in the same counterproductive manner as were his and his subordinates' public conversation.

The use of self-induced censorship in order to create conditions for dialogue is rarely successful. For example, when some of the professionals were asked if they had any idea of their bosses' private thoughts, they responded with words that were almost identical to the ones the

CIO used. When they were asked what led them not to say so, they responded with the same look of astonishment. 'Are you kidding', said one of them, 'that would make things worse.'

Reflecting on the action of the CIO and his immediate reports

The CIO decided to begin the meeting with a 'take charge' attitude. He told his group about negative evaluations by the top, and warned them that the time had come for corrective action. He then requested a constructive dialogue about what could be done to correct the situation. The subordinates also had their own 'take charge' attitude. They bypassed the CIO's request, arguing that the problems were caused by top management.

The CIO responded in two ways. First, he avoided publicly expressing his negative feelings, fearing that doing so could make the situation worse. I would agree. If he were to make public his negative evaluations and attributions, he would be likely to activate the same kind of defensiveness that his subordinates' negative evaluations and attributions had activated in him. The very way he framed his private thoughts and feelings was counterproductive to learning. The irony was that his private thoughts were consistent with the views of the CEO. For example, both saw the IT professionals as uncooperative and acting childishly.

Thus the first action strategy the CIO used in the name of producing a positive dialogue increased the amount of information that was withheld, suppressed his personal feelings, bypassed the feelings of his subordinates, and acted as if he was not doing so.

The second way the CIO responded was to take a rational approach to the problem. He asked the group to develop a credible plan to respond to the need of line management. The subordinates rejected this suggestion on grounds that it was irrational: the line managers did not know how to plan, were not likely to be satisfied with a sound plan, and would only escalate their demands and criticisms.

So far, all three levels of participants seem to have the same strategy. All believe that they should take charge and warn others that their actions are not acceptable. This activates a barrage of evaluations and attributions on all sides, crafted in ways that do not encourage learning. For example, the subordinates evaluate the line as unable to plan and attribute to them the intention of making life difficult for the IT group. The CIO privately felt the same about the IT group but decided that in order to have a constructive discussion he should remain rational and focus on developing new plans. Again, he appears to be struggling to remain at the rational level of planning, suppressing his private thoughts and feelings, in order to avoid provoking emotional responses that he sees as unconstructive.

The result of all this was direct and straightforward: it protected the status quo, at least for the short run. No one in the IT group would have to try new behavior.

Case 6: Advanced MBAs

A group of second year MBAs tackled a case about work compensation. The instructor asked Mary to begin the discussion. Mary began by stating that she was against group bonus plans and in favor of individual incentive plans. Examples of statements that Mary made include:

I recommend that we abolish group bonus plans. I don't like them. We cannot produce enough (using group plans).

Group incentives are unfair. They encourage malingering. I want to get rid of them.

The employees do not understand the cost accounting behind incentive plans. (They do not really understand what is in their best interest!)

The instructor asked Mary how she would implement her views with the union leaders. Mary replied:

I am confident that (my plan) will give the workers incentives to work harder.

I'll call in the union leaders to see what they think. I would get their support for my views.

They'll like what I have to say because they will realize that they will make more money. I fully believe that (my plan will give them what they want).

The instructor asked Mary to reflect on how the union leaders would react to what she just said. Mary responded that she would be 'careful' in how she talked with the leaders. She realized that they may not agree with her position. But, she added, now is the time to take action that would solve the cost problem in manufacturing.

Mary's causal theory of effective action when she was talking to her classmates or to the union leaders included the following reasoning.

If I advocate my views with genuine enthusiasm,
If I do not encourage confrontation of my views,
If I censor potentially upsetting views, and feelings,
If I act as if I am not censoring these thoughts and feelings,
Then I will win over the others, classmates and union leaders.

Some students who disagreed with Mary

When Mary's position was thrown open for discussion, the strongest disagreement was that her position would harm workers with seniority who have been team players for years. For example:

Student 1: Yes I'm for seniority. When you are new or young you are willing to work your butt off. I realize that my plan would not work for everyone. But (I feel sure) that (this is the way to go).

Student 2: I'm surprised with the support for seniority. I'm surprised because we are advising that we make it easier. I think it is important to go for (meritocracy). We have to be able to say that the easier strategy is not necessarily the correct one.

Student 3: I disagree with (Student 2) in every respect [*class laughter*]. The firms that are making money are using seniority for competitive advantage. The reason for seniority is that if you get rid of intrinsic rewards like loyalty you will kill the firm.

Student 4: I disagree with you. The real reason that we want to emphasize meritocracy is...Turning to seniority is a mistake. You will attract mediocre people (and then you will be in trouble).

Student 5: Yes I think you're *wrong*. [*Class laughter and student gets up as if to leave.*] Sorry about that. I agree with (Student 4) very strongly.

A summary of the major action strategies and reasoning processes used by the participants

Be strong, persuade, and sell. Deflect or ignore contrary views. Expect others to trust your views and the reasoning behind them. Polarize the positions, then take one and defend it by being articulate and strong. Express views with strong emotions. As one student said, 'We revved it up a bit.' Provide reasons, to support one's own position, that are subjective views, untested attributions, and undocumented conclusions. Do not encourage inquiry into any of the above.

The students' actions to lead and influence others may be said to have two components. The first is to convince others by acting with conviction of the validity of their claims. As they produce their sense of conviction, they also become intransigent.

There is a fundamental problem with the conviction–intransigence pattern. If this strategy is implemented it requires others to become submissive. The others cannot act with conviction and intransigence without escalating the counterproductive consequences of creating a Trap.

Conclusion

The cases presented in this chapter show that the behavior exhibited at the State Department and Intel is in fact ubiquitous. We entrap ourselves all the time—all the while thinking we are doing the best we can to solve problems effectively. Anyone with any experience at all with human conflict should recognize the problems presented here.

This behavior creates Traps that cause massive errors. Errors are mismatches between what is intended and what actually happens:

1. Actions intended to increase openness, transparency, and trust often create the opposite.

2. We want to bring up a problem but submerge it in focusing on something else.

3. Whenever differences and complications arise, people blame others and the system. They rarely are aware of their actions that create Traps.

4. Upward and downward communications about difficult issues are often lacking.

5. We try to change but behave in ways that support the status quo.

Why do we behave this way? Is it because human beings are just incompetent in many different ways? On the contrary, as I will show in the next chapter, human beings are very competent at producing this behavior, are skilled at it, and in fact, are skilled in being unaware of what they are doing.

3

Causes of Traps

In Chapter 1, I presented two broad-brush cases involving Dean Rusk at the State Department and Andrew Grove at Intel, which showed how these very talented and accomplished men became ensnared in traps of their own making. To show that these cases were far from exceptional, in Chapter 2 I presented cases from a range of ordinary people who describe *in their own words* how they failed to achieve the results they intended—and in fact often reinforced the status quo. For example, the supervisor in the first case was concerned that the subordinate wasn't taking responsibility—but never brought that issue up, and instead focused on technical issues. In another case, a CIO could not get his direct reports to consider any changes whatsoever, even though the CIO knew his job was on the line. In all the cases people kept thoughts and feelings hidden, thinking that such self-censorship was necessary to have productive conversations.

Why do human beings produce the sorts of results I have documented—results that are *counterproductive to their own stated interests and intentions*? Why do they seem unaware that they are producing the counterproductive consequences while doing so? Why if pressed to become aware do they deny their personal causal responsibility followed by denying that they are denying? Why, if pressing continues, do they claim that they are victims of the actions of others? Why do they express a sense of helplessness? Why do they express a sincere doubt that these patterns are correctable—that is, a sense of being in a Trap.

This chapter presents a theory that is intended to explain these puzzling and seemingly inexplicable patterns. Our theory begins with the premise that all action is designed and implemented by human beings with the intention to produce a desired result. In many cases, when our actions do not produce the desired result, we learn to change our actions. For example, when learning to drive a car, if we step on the brake and almost go through the windshield, we learn to apply pressure to the brake more gradually. This sort of learning is routine and ubiquitous—except in certain situations, situations such as those encountered by the people in the examples I have presented.

The people in the examples are not facing inanimate objects such as a car, but other human beings in situations that are to some extent uncertain and ambiguous. Dean Rusk, for example, is not sure how his senior ambassadors will respond to his request for openness and transparency. He moves cautiously, because the uncertainty makes the situation threatening. For their part, the ambassadors definitely see the request as threatening, potentially leading to 'career suicide', as we saw. In the case of the boss who wanted to ease his subordinate off the product development committee, the boss was uncertain about the employee's reaction. He wanted to take away the committee membership while maintaining the subordinate's commitment and motivation to her current job. He felt this was a delicate situation that had to be approached carefully.

What makes situations that are potentially threatening or embarrassing different is that human beings react to them in ways that inhibit learning. They react to them in ways that will reduce or remove the threat and potential embarrassment. Ostensibly, the people in the cases we have examined are trying to produce openness and transparency (in the case of Rusk and Grove), find ways to increase learning (in the case of the financial officers) and increase cooperation (in the case of the CIO and the IT department), yet not one of these objectives is achieved.

What are we to say about all these people, the CIO, the financial officers, Andrew Grove, Dean Rusk, and all the rest who are unable to achieve the results they say they want? Were their failings few and far between, we could chalk them up to bad luck or perhaps carelessness. But they are consistent and persistent. As noted, we have now documented more than 10,000 cases that display similar patterns—patterns in which people end up trapped. Are we to say that human beings are thoroughly incompetent?

It is not that people are incompetent in achieving the results they desire—in fact they are quite competent: *but what they are competent at is avoiding threatening and embarrassing situations.*

If this is true then we must have rules in our heads that lead us to:

1. Produce consequences that we do not intend when dealing with difficult problems.
2. Hold other people or the system responsible for errors and not examine our own responsibility.
3. Repeat errors skillfully so that they can continue to be repeated.
4. Create organizational black holes in which information is driven underground.

Whenever I state these rules, executives express disbelief that they actually hold them. We need a theory that explains where the rules come from, the disbelief of the actors that they use such rules, and their unawareness that they are doing so.

To make sense of these puzzles, we need to explain two things. First, people use theories of action to produce intended results and the theories they use and the theories they *say* they use may be different. In other words theories-in-use are not the same as espoused theories. Second, there are two models of reasoning, defensive reasoning (we call it Model I) and productive reasoning (Model II).

A Theory of Action

The theory of action that I propose is based on the premise that human beings create designs for action that specify the actions we need to undertake to get what we want.

They specify strategies for resolving conflicts, making a living, closing a deal—for every sort of purpose we try to achieve. We store these designs and activate them whenever needed.

The human mind organizes these designs into a master program for how to act effectively. There are two kinds of master programs. One describes the theory of action that human beings espouse. That is, people believe they act on the principles of this theory and when asked about it, say they use it. The second is the theory that they actually use: their theory-in-use. It is possible that a person's espoused theory and theory-in-use match in every detail. However, this is not a given: consider the almost universal parental injunction, 'Do as I say, not as I do.' (Thus, people may say they believe in telling the truth, being fair, and following the golden rule even when in practice they often hide the truth, act with bias, and seek unilateral advantage.) And in the cases we have been looking at, it is apparent that the individuals' espoused theories and theories-in-use diverge in significant ways.

Early in our research my colleagues and I did not expect that individuals would implement a theory-in-use that was significantly different from their espoused theory, nor did we expect them to be unaware of the inconsistency when the theory they implemented was different from their espoused theory. Therefore it was a major surprise to find that there are often fundamental, systematic mismatches between individuals' espoused theories of action and their actual theories in use.

It is the theory-in-use combined with a reasoning mind-set that explains the puzzles described above and that we will use to diagnose and reduce Traps. What is this theory-in-use and the mind-set that accompanies it?

Model I theory-in-use: defensive reasoning[1]

After examining thousands of left-hand–right-hand cases and observing people in action in all sorts of situations, I have concluded that four values govern the actions of human beings:

1. Be in unilateral control.
2. Win and do not lose.
3. Suppress negative feelings.
4. Behave rationally.

The purpose of Model I is to protect and defend the self against fundamental, disruptive change. As human beings become skillful in using Model I, they develop a defensive reasoning mind-set that they use to explain their actions and to design and implement future actions. Model I reasoning represents our theory-in-use when we face threatening or potentially embarrassing situations.

---

[1] Recent thoughtful books describing research and intervention that are consistent with a theory of design and a theory of action are Boonstra and Caluwe (2007), Clark and Myers (2007), Lipchitz *et al.* (2007), Manzoni and Barsoux (2002), Mazen (1997), Noonan (2007), Romme and Georges (2003), Schmidt (2005, 2006), Smith (2008), Van Aken *et al.* (2007).

However, there is another theory that people espouse, which is Model II productive reasoning.

Model II theory-in-use: productive reasoning

Model II is a theory-in-use that can be used to begin to prevent the counterproductive consequence of Model I. Model II theories are, at the outset, espoused theories. The challenge is to help individuals transform the espoused theories into theories-in-use by learning a new set of skills and a new set of governing values. Because many individuals espouse Model II values and skills, these traits are not totally new to them. However, the empirical fact to date is that very few individuals can routinely act on their espoused values, and they are often unaware of this limitation.

The governing values of Model II are:

1. Seek valid (testable) information.
2. Create informed choice.
3. Monitor vigilantly to detect and correct error.

As individuals become skillful at using Model II, they will also become skillful at using productive reasoning. Productive reasoning can be used to make personal reasoning transparent in order for the claims to be tested robustly. In order to develop a productive reasoning mind-set, it is necessary to become skillful at producing Model II governing values. Model II governing values can lead to openness, transparency, and trust. However, empirical evidence shows that few people have a Model II theory-in-use.

How We Create Traps

The problem—and the reason we create Traps for ourselves—is that we espouse Model II reasoning when our actions are in fact based on Model I. Thus, we think we are acting in a way that creates trust, informed choice, and valid information, but in fact, we are acting in ways that undermine those values in order to defend the self. Let's look more closely at some of the cases we have previously discussed.

The State Department

Recall that Rusk's espoused intentions were to get more openness, transparency, and trust in the interactions among those at the highest level of the State Department—in other words, he was hoping to get people to use Model II and productive reasoning. However, his actions during the meeting were consistent with Model I theory-in-use. For example, he strove to be in control by advocating his position rationally and promising to champion the new modes of communication.

As soon as he sensed the lukewarm response to what he was advocating he decided that if he was not careful he could lose control over the meeting and thus lose rather than win. So instead of pressing the issue and risking overt resistance, he allowed the session to end inconclusively, with tepid support from only one participant. He increased the likelihood of suppressing negative feelings by suppressing his own negative feelings and acting as if he was not. He also suppressed his strategy to use the senior ambassador to support him and by using me to express openly what was undiscussable, namely that the senior officials were likely to resist the programs and to act as if they were not.

In addition to advocating his position, Rusk was actively evaluating the responses of the ambassadors. He judged that the responses were negative. He did not make these evaluations transparent and risk losing rather than winning and therefore he could not test their validity. Rusk also made attributions that the ambassadors would not support the program. Yet, he did not strive to test his attribution publicly. There was little transparency on his part or on the part of the ambassadors. All were using Model I governing values and action strategies that led to such consequences as creating undiscussables.

The participants also used Model I defensive reasoning. They acted skillfully to drive the counterproductive actions underground and they acted as if they were not doing so. Several of the participants told me at the end of the meeting that they felt relieved that the Secretary did not strive to make discussable what they all 'knew' was really going on. The senior ambassador 'knew' that is how the participants felt. He reasoned that it would be inappropriate to state these feelings publicly during the meeting. But he promised to be candid with the Secretary during a private dinner. I wondered if the ambassador 'knew' that the Secretary would feel shocked by the ambassador's action and that he would consider being open with the ambassador was inappropriate.

Intel

Grove espoused that effective leadership was composed of a combination of hard work, rigorous reasoning, technical competence, and courage. As we have seen, the subordinates believed in the value of these features. They espoused features that supported the concept of enthusiastic adherence to rationality. The belief was that under these conditions all would be in control and would win.

Unfortunately, these conditions were not enough to deal with disagreements between the subordinates and Grove. He acted so as to be in control and to win by behaving in ways that suppressed the subordinates from pushing back. The rules for dealing with Grove's leadership style were undiscussable and their undiscussability undiscussable.

The cover-up features of these action strategies were partially legitimized, in the eyes of the subordinates, because Grove ruled out discussions of leadership style. Grove acted openly and with transparency to rule out openness and transparency by making the rules undiscussable.

Grove on the other hand believed that he was open about what he believed was effective leadership. (He believed he was acting on his Model II espoused theory, when in fact his theory-in-use was Model I.) He was transparent about what would happen if his rules were not followed. Where Rusk sought to encourage dialogue about style and interpersonal communication, Grove did not. He simply ruled it out. They acted differently yet they followed the governing values of their respective theories-in-use, namely Model I.

S and O submerging the primary issue

Recall that in this case S's doubt about O's performance is driven by S's belief that O avoids taking responsibility to solve the technical problems, but that S talks only about technical issues and does not bring up his concerns about O's personal responsibility. Now let's look at what sort of conversation S and O might have had if S had not tried to hide his real concern about O's personal responsibility for the late delivery of his team's projects (see Table 3.1).

O could respond to S's initiative by cooperating in two ways. First, he could answer S's attributions that O was avoiding responsibility. Second, he might also admit he covered up these feelings by focusing on the technical issues and by covering up the cover-up. S could then ask O to describe his fears. Such inquiry often enlarges the issue from an interpersonal one to one that includes relevant organizational factors, and show how two kinds of factors reinforce each other. The participants are now on their way to more productive learning about technical interpersonal and organizational binds in which they have been caught up.

But the key question here is, why does S not proceed in this way? S's left-hand column shows feelings and thoughts that are not disclosed to O in any way. Why is S uncomfortable with expressing his thoughts and doubts as he does in my imagined second case? One reason might be that it feels threatening to reveal his own doubts about

Table 3.1. Conversation and reasoning

What S could say	The reasoning behind the design
O: I would like to discuss with you a problem that continues between us. (*Describes problem.*) I am bewildered how to resolve it effectively.	Seek to test view of the problem. Seek to discover possible personal responsibility.
Every time I raise the issue about on-time delivery, you claim the cause is due to the computer/ debugger interaction.	Reflect on some segments of dialogue that S uses to infer the problem.
I react in two ways. One way is to attribute to you that you are avoiding the problem. I do not test this attribution.	Make private attributions public. Own up that S does not test.
The other way is that I craft most of my responses at the technical level. This appears, to me, to make it easier for you to respond at the technical level. It also makes it more difficult for me to deal with the issue that troubles me.	Make his private attributions public in order to test them. Own up to the realization that the process S uses is counterproductive.
In the name of being positive, I hide all of this, but, as far as I can tell, the results are not positive.	Make public his covered-up actions. Own up to the dysfunctionality of these actions.
Does this diagnosis make sense to you? If not, where do you differ?	Ask for test.
If it does make sense, would you be willing to join me in redesigning the way we deal with each other?	Invites the joint design and implementation of more constructive actions.

how to proceed. Another could be that proceeding along the imagined conversation gives O a good deal of control over the conversation. In the actual case, S doesn't express his real concerns, but does manage to maintain control of the conversation and keep it from going into areas that may make S uncomfortable. Notice too how unreal the above conversation seems. In real life we seldom hear people reveal this level of self-disclosure or this level of doubt. This shows how prevalent defensive reasoning is.

Indeed, this sort of behavior is endemic to Traps.

The CIO and the IT department

In this case, recall that in the face of demands from the CEO for improved productivity, the CIO met with his top reports to find a response. Although the group expressed an interest in solving the business problem, their ways of crafting their conversation, combined with their self-censorship, led to a dialogue that was defensive and self-reinforcing. As we have argued, conditions for productive inquiry are highly unlikely when people use Model I theories-in-use. How might the CIO have led the conversation, using a productive reasoning mind-set?

To make Model II and productive reasoning more than an espoused theory, the challenge is to create a dialogue, assumptions can be reformulated, incongruities reconciled, incompatibilities resolved, vagueness specified, untestable notions made testable, scattered information brought together into meaningful patterns, and previously with-held information surfaced.

The basic thrust of CIO's conversation would have to be toward making issues more explicit and testing the valid-ity of assumptions and attributions related to them, in order to enhance productive learning. When the CIO hears his subordinates say that the line managers 'do not know what they want' he might carry on the following conversation with himself:

These individuals are making evaluations of and attributions about the line's intentions without providing any data that I (or anyone else) could use to make up my own mind about the validity of their claims.

I should ask them to provide data to illustrate their claims. I have learned not to ask them 'why' they believe what they do, because that will activate espoused-theory explanations that are likely to be self serving. Rather than ask for their theories, I should ask them to focus on hard evidence.

When the subordinates say that line managers don't know what they want, I should say, 'What is it that they say or do that leads you to conclude that they do not know what they want?'

If this question is answered concretely, the CIO can make a judgment as to whether line managers are acting inappropriately. If they are, in his judgment, he can communicate these evaluations upward in order to begin to change line managers' actions.

Let us consider another example for the CIO's dialogue with his subordinates. When the subordinates say that line does not trust them or really care for them, the CIO could say, 'Have you tested out your assumptions about their views of us? If so, what did you say to the line? If not, what led you not to do so?'

If the CIO asks these questions, the subordinates might say 'Are you kidding? That would be disastrous. They would either laugh or get furious.' *Their response is another attribution about the line management.* As such, it should be tested by the use of a logic that is different from the one used by the information technology professionals themselves. If all the CIO hears are further untested assertions, he could say something like, 'I ask if you have tested the validity of your assertions. I cannot be an effective representative of our views with line management if I come to the meetings armed with untestable assertions.'

If the CIO hears what he believes are incorrect or self-sealing conclusions, he could ask:

If it is true that the users are the problem, because they do not plan and they make last minute demands and if it is also true that they have been doing this for years, and if we got increased resources, would that not reinforce the very behavior we find frustrating?

Or

You tell me that our clients are inflexible and insensitive. That may be true. But how do you know? The only answer I get when I ask you this question is that you say they are ... [*illustrates with examples of what the subordinates have said*]. I would like these attributions and evaluations to be tested in ways that are independent of your reasoning. Otherwise, I could put myself in the position of being seen as an uncritical carrier of IT self-justifications.

I cannot go along with causal reasoning, yours or mine, when validity is not tested independently of our views, experiences, and logic.

The CIO could also cite actions that illustrate how his subordinates may be creating the very consequences they condemn. He might say:

You state that our customers are inflexible and insensitive [*cites illustrations of such claims*]. You do not like this behavior, and you use it as evidence that the problems are not correctable.

You may be right, but I do not hear anyone presenting a compelling argument that is also testable. Whenever I have tried to make some suggestions, the responses that I hear from you include 'good luck to you' and 'trust us' our users are uninfluenceable.

It is difficult for me to trust your diagnosis. If you act toward the line managers the way you are acting toward me, I can see how they would become, in your eyes, uninfluenceable. But I can also see how they may come to a similar conclusion about you.

The upshot of such a conversation might be very uncomfortable—which is why it is usually avoided in favor of Model I and defensive reasoning—but facing uncomfortable truths is often the prerequisite for real change.

The MBA students

The MBA students also followed the same governing values. Their action strategies were to advocate their views, to make evaluations of others' views and attributions. They crafted these in ways that led to a pattern of conviction and intransigence. They did not invite discussion of the counterproductive features of their pattern. Indeed, they supported its use by saying that it was a sign of strong leadership. They did not discuss this claim publicly because it was considered inappropriate by the instructor and by the rules he promulgated about effective classroom behavior.

How Model I Theory-in-Use and Defensive Reasoning Lead to Traps

We can now see how the Model I theory-in-use and defensive reasoning lead to Traps. Model I, defensive reasoning, and Traps that create counterproductive and ineffective action are activated where the problems being dealt with are wicked and dangerous. This means that Traps are not as likely to be activated where the problems are not threatening the status quo. However, once the Traps are established, they reinforce each other in a manner that is self-fueling. The self-fueling and self-sealing features lead individuals to doubt that Traps can be changed. The actors claim that they cannot correct these conditions because they are not to blame. They are victims; they are helpless (defensive reasoning).

So far, the theories-in-use that inform behavior are the same in all cultures, organizations, or communities as well as gender, race, wealth, and education (Argyris 1982, 1985, 1990, 1993; Argyris *et al.* 1985; Argyris and Schön 1996). Does this mean a Model III or IV does not exist? No, it only means that neither we nor anyone else has discovered it. But we do take the position that Model I and II are adequate to explain, diagnose, and begin to change Traps. But this claim is subject to test.

There is another issue about variance. We claim that there is variance in the actual behavior of espoused theory and theory-in-use. We also claim that any actions observed to be informed by Model I may vary but not beyond Model I. Thus the actions by Rusk, Grove, and the students varied widely but never beyond Model I.

How can we explain the fact that human beings are unaware of gaps and inconsistencies that they are producing when they use Model I and defensive reasoning? If they create these designs how come they are unaware when they are using them?

The answer is itself paradoxical. They are unaware because they have become skillful at producing them. In order for Model I and defensive reasoning to be produced, human beings have to practice both to the point where they are highly skilled. Then, the actions, and the reasoning associated with them, become spontaneous and taken for granted. They become tacit. Once they become tacit people no longer pay attention to them, hence the unawareness while taking action. They may become quite aware when they are questioned by others or if they question themselves. But the questioning cannot be crafted consistently with Model I because it will be counterproductive to the learning that is necessary. The point is that unawareness is caused by becoming skillful.

This process is similar to learning how to ride a bike. At the start, one thinks about how to keep one's balance, which way to lean in turns, and the like. But when one succeeds at learning how to ride, one ceases to think about the process; it becomes habitual. Indeed, thinking about it can impair one's ability to actually do it. Similarly, using a Model I theory-in-use effectively requires the actor not to think about doing so.

Some confusion about Traps

Some executives and consultants who note that Traps are self-fueling and self-sealing conclude that this indicates the existence of psychological defensive routines that may require therapy to correct. It is true that Traps are anti-learning and persistently so. These are the same features of neurotic behavior described in the clinical literature. The similarity ends there.

Our concept of Traps contains features that differ importantly from the clinical versions. The clinical trap results in clients who express suffering, pain, and hurt. The causes of these negative consequences are typically thought to begin early in the lives of clients especially during their interactions with parents. There is a long and robust literature on theories of how neurotic behavior is produced. The causes are often manifested in a pattern that is unique to the individual involved.

The actors (think Rusk, Grove, and MBA students) do not report personal psychological suffering and pain. They may express a sense of sadness that is often followed up with the view 'that's life in organizations'. They do not see themselves as weak. The leadership strategies that they use are seen as necessary in order to get the job done. The causes are to be found in the 'here and now' not in their personal historical past.

A second possible source of misunderstanding is equating the social psychological concept of 'cognitive dissonance' with Traps. Again, there are the similarities described above. There are however, some important differences. Human beings, this theory asserts, spend much effort in justifying their actions, especially when their predictions are falsified. A premise of this theory is that self-justification is at the heart of cognitive dissonance (Tavris and Aronson 2007). The engine that drives self-justification is the mental discomfort that they experience when their predictions are falsified and when their reasoning is questioned. Individuals do not rest easy until the mental discomfort is reduced.

Self-justification is not the same thing as lying or making excuses. Self-justification is lying to one's self. This is why the authors contend that 'self justification is more powerful and more dangerous than the explicit lie. It allows people to convince themselves that what they did was the best thing they could have done' (Tavris and Aronson 2007: 14). Their reasoning is that their actions represented a brilliant solution or that they represented the best interest of all concerned.

In the case of Traps, individuals also rationalize their actions as acting in the best interests of all concerned. However, the source of their actions is not some type of mental disorder that must be reduced. The actions are justified by human beings following the behavioral demands of Traps. They do not report a personal sense of mental discomfort. Indeed, by adhering to these behavioral demands they are able to deny personal causal responsibility, deny that they are denying, and be skillfully unaware. In the short run, Traps create more comfort than discomfort.

Finally, if self-justification is behavior, it must be produced by designs-in-use stored in our mind/brain. The designs-in-use are created as human beings become skillful at self-justification. How do human beings learn to become skillful at self-justification? Our suggestion is that they learn to be skillful by the same processes they learn to act skillfully in producing Traps. They learn a Model I theory-in-use and a defensive resoning mind-set. The learning is approved through organizational defenses and social virtues. Self-justification is not lying to one's self. It is activating Traps.

Conclusion

In conclusion, Traps emerge and persist when individuals use Model I theory-in-use and defensive reasoning. They cause skilled incompetence, skilled unawareness, and self-protective actions such as denial of denying, and making issues undiscussable, including the undiscussability of the undiscussable.

Traps entangle not only individuals, but also groups, relations between groups, and entire organizations. For example, many organizations have developed norms that encourage distancing and helplessness to take corrective actions.

In order to reduce Traps, we must begin by addressing Model I theories-in-use and defensive reasoning. Traps cannot be reduced by focusing on environmental factors such as new structures and reward policies. Individuals operating in such structures or under such policies will use the theory-in-use that they already hold and the defensive reasoning they use to protect themselves.

For example, Burns and Stalker (1961) described mechanistic and organic organizations. The former were consistent with Model I theory-in-use and defensive reasoning. The latter were consistent with Model II theory-in-use and productive reasoning. The individuals who were in organic structures were never educated in Model II theory-in-use and productive reasoning. We would predict that whenever these individuals discussed technical or human problems they would use the only theory-in-use they had, namely, Model I. The authors provided a few pages of actual conversation of some difficult issues. An analysis of three transcripts indicates that they were Model I (Argyris 1980), thus the actual behavior was consistent with mechanistic organization even though the structure was organic.

This inconsistency continues to flourish. In the chapters in Part II on effective leadership, cultural change, and new organizational designs I show how leading researchers focus upon many factors but not on the theories-in-use and reasoning mind-sets. The advice offered is not implementable when it bypasses the existence of Traps.

Part II

How Conventional Approaches Bypass Traps—and What to Do About it

Introduction

In the previous chapters we have seen that Traps exist throughout organizations and affect people at all levels, all backgrounds, and both sexes. Traps are patterns of actions and reasoning that, when implemented, make it difficult to produce the learning that is required to generate fundamental change. Such patterns include, for example, censoring one's thoughts, denying that one is doing so, making problematic behavior or norms undiscussable and that undiscussability itself taboo, and blaming others. All these combine to produce a victim mentality and a genuine belief that reducing Traps is hopeless, romantic, and unrealistic. We feel stuck, trapped in the status quo. This defensive reasoning 'protects' Model I theory-in-use which in turn feeds back to reinforce the Trap pattern. Traps become self-reinforcing, self-fueling. As noted in the Introduction (pp. 1–2), we end up saying such things as:

They just don't want to hear the truth.

You just can't talk to them honestly—they immediately get defensive.

We all agreed in the meeting, but of course, nothing will come of it.

She ran the meeting as if it would be a group decision, but really she had already made up her mind.

Of course I couldn't say that to his face.

Nothing will ever change.

Finally, we have seen that people themselves are responsible for making the status quo so resistant to change. We are *not* victims. We are trapped by our own behavior. Interventions are available that interrupt these self-fueling, self-reinforcing, self-sealing processes to begin to reduce the Traps. The interventions begin with diagnosing the participants' Model I theory-in-use and defensive reasoning (left-hand–right-hand case). They continue until the denials (and the denials of the denials) are acknowledged as counterproductive. Model II theory-in use and productive reasoning are then introduced and applied to reducing the Traps described above.

The intervention is relatively straightforward. The most critical features are genuine commitment to learning Model II and productive reasoning, coupled with time to practice. It takes as much practice to begin to become skillful as it does to become skillful at playing a moderately good game of tennis.

The good news is that the practice is most likely to be effective if it occurs in the context of real problems faced by the participants. This practice is integrated with actual problems faced by individuals, groups, inter-groups, and organizations. If the interventions are effective, the participants will not say, 'we have no time for this stuff, we have real problems to solve', because they are striving to solve 'real' problems.

However, much of the literature on improving organizational performance and effectiveness, on leading change, and on personal transformation bypasses the problems of Traps—and in doing so, ignores the very thing that makes change so difficult. In the next three chapters I focus on what some of the best known literature tells us about how to increase leadership effectiveness (Chapter 4), how to produce cultures that reinforce new concepts of performance (Chapter 5), and how to implement new concepts of organizational design (Chapter 6).

Although the advice in these chapters is created by a diverse group of researchers and thoughtful practitioners, they have one feature in common: namely that, for most of them, the distinction between espoused theory and theory-in-use is not a central component of their theory of explanation and intervention. They do not deny that this distinction is relevant. They choose not to focus their work upon it.

This stance influences how we provide an evaluation that is valid and yet opens itself to being critiqued by the readers. Our strategy was as follows. Our critique should be based upon what the writers claim are fundamental features of their advice. For example, we begin the critique of leadership by quoting examples of their advice as to how to produce more effective leadership. We then examine the examples to identify gaps and inconsistencies that appear not to be recognized by the writers.

One gap that is found in most of the literature is that the advice is given as abstract ideas based upon espoused theory data. We then ask the respective advisers how they would translate advice that excludes theory-in-use prescriptions. For example, we identify advice that leaders should be more effective at being inspirational. In order to do so the leaders should display enthusiasm and optimism. This advice does not inform us how leaders can make it attainable. Nor does it tell us how leaders who are not enthusiastic and optimistic can become more so, if they wish to act in these ways.

Another type of inquiry that we conduct is to identify issues that are relevant in making the advice more valid. For example, we could ask, if Rusk and Grove believe they are appropriately committed and enthusiastic about changing leadership effectiveness, how would they explain that their two leadership styles are contradictory? Also how come these contradictory leadership styles produce the same counterproductive consequences, namely, reinforcing Traps?

The intent of the reviews is to illuminate gaps and inconsistencies that the respective authors do not make explicit. Hopefully this may stimulate interest in examining any flaws in the advice. It also may activate the readers of the advice to identify gaps and inconsistencies that have been made explicit. New awareness could help the users of the advice to prepare themselves to deal with problems that may arise that the advisers have not made explicit.

4

Leadership and Traps

Most of us, even our best and brightest leaders such as Dean Rusk and Andrew Grove, live in a Model I world even while we espouse Model II values. In other words, we say we value open inquiry, testable knowledge, and informed choice, but we act to maintain unilateral control, to ensure that we win, to rule topics undiscussable, and then deny that we are doing all this. To put it more bluntly, we may espouse Model II action strategies, but we do not have the skills to produce them—as the cases previously discussed demonstrate. Moreover, as I have argued, we are unaware that this is the case—skillfully so. (Analogously, a person with deep racial prejudices may espouse racial tolerance, but be unable to demonstrate it through personal actions and remain unaware of this limitation.)

Given this universal human predicament, how can we learn to change, to improve our leadership, when both we and those we interact with are trapped in a Model I world, when we censor our true thoughts, blame others for problems, make topics undiscussable, and that undiscussability off limits? If, as I have suggested, we use Model I as our Theory in Action to shield us from threatening truths and protect us from uncomfortable change, it would seem that leadership experts who offer advice on improving leadership face a daunting task. For their advice to be appreciated and implemented by leaders it must not be threatening—and so cannot be more than superficial. On the other hand, advice intended to produce truly new levels of leadership will require significant personal change—and so not be implementable by those with a Model I theory-in-use and a defensive reasoning mind-set.

The first purpose of this chapter is to answer the question, what advice would those seeking to reduce Traps get by reading the research on leadership written by some of our most celebrated and widely read researchers and experts. Is it useful? Is it implementable? As we will see, readers will find little advice on how to reduce Traps that is implementable. Why is this so? Individuals seeking to act more effectively, especially to diagnose and reduce Traps, need to know their theory-in-use and the degree to which they use a defensive reasoning mind-set. They also need to know the degree to which they blame others, deny their personal causal responsibilities. They also need to know how Traps become self-fueling and self-sealing, and that defensive reasoning is helpless to reduce Traps.

No advice for dealing with such issues is given. Moreover, as we read their advice we will see that it reads as if the inconsistencies between their espoused theories and Model I theory-in-use do not exist. Or, if they do, they are not important. For example, the advice reads as if the meaning of caring and concern is the same for everyone. Indeed, it is. The respondents use Model I and defensive reasoning, yet they seek Model II actions.

Another problem that arises where there is no distinction made between espoused theories and theories-in-use is that the researchers provide advice that they believe is actionable when it is not. This leads to the second purpose of the chapter. I seek to show that the works of the researchers reviewed in this book bypass the problem of reducing Traps because of the most fundamental assumptions they hold about effective research.

I organize my review around research that is quantitative and research that is qualitative. I do so because the supporters of each stream make claims that their emphasis will produce more effective results. I will show that, as far as Traps are concerned, the two streams produce knowledge that is incomplete and lacks implementable validity. The same is true for changing culture (Chapter 5) and for designing new modes of designing and managing organizations (Chapter 6).

The Quantitative Approach

I begin with the research on transformational and transactional leaders. The primary methodology is the use of various types of questionnaires and surveys coupled with a secondary emphasis upon interviews and documents that describe leaders' actions. The researchers (such as

Bass and Riggio 2006; Avolio 2007; Avolio and Bass 2004) seek to establish a high degree of validity by analyzing their questions rigorously before they are used in actual studies. They also focus on using appropriate sample sizes. The samples used are critical because the researchers assume that meaningful samples will reduce threats to the validity of their findings. This assumption is based on another, namely that there is a wide degree of variance in how people behave. Without a degree of variance they cannot establish the largely correlational analysis that they make.

There are two problems with these assumptions when it comes to producing actionable advice. The first problem is that the data they use are espoused theory data. As we have amply demonstrated, one's espoused theory can be very different from one's actual theory-in-use. Recall that Rush and Grove exposed different views of effective action. However, they used the same theory-in-use. The researchers do not focus on the theories-in-use of their respondents. If they had, they would find no variance.

To improve effectiveness, these researchers advise leaders to develop skills at using idealized influence, inspirational motivation, individualized consideration, and intellectual stimulation. Idealized influence is defined as the leader emphasizing a collective sense of mission, and reassuring others that the obstacles they face can be overcome. Inspirational motivation means that the leaders strive to motivate others to their position by displaying enthusiasm and optimism. Intellectual stimulation means that leaders educate others to what excellence means.

These meanings are further operationalized in the comprehensive diagnostic notebooks that leaders are asked to complete in order to understand their leadership.

The advice above begins at the most abstract level and expands as they go along. For example, they advise that leaders should be skillful at producing inspirational motivation. The user can produce this by motivating others. They motivate others by displaying enthusiasm and optimism.

Rusk believed that he exhibited enthusiasm and optimism. So did Grove. Yet their actual behavior differed. The MBA students believed that they acted with enthusiasm. They also did so by combining the enthusiasm with intransigence because they believed that pattern showed strong leadership.

Avolio advises leaders to act integratively. Integrative leaders 'somehow gets their immediate followers to successfully assume a leadership role' (2007: 29). They do so by such actions as building the followers' competence to exercise greater responsibility. Effective leaders seek to identify followers who are capable of identifying their core strengths. As the followers become skillful at these actions, they demonstrate their willingness to assume increased responsibility, which the leader reinforces through feedback and recognition, completing the cycle for development.

In order for users to implement the Avolio advice they would have (1) to specify how to produce actions that 'somehow' get subordinates to successfully assume leadership, (2) to believe that they are capable of doing so, and (3) to believe that they can establish mutually developing relationships. The CIO whose job was on the line in the case presented in Chapter 2 was desperate to achieve such results with his team. Is there anything useful here for him? By what actions does a leader 'signal' to subordinates that they are capable of accelerating their performance? What are the actions that followers use to demonstrate their willingness to take personal responsibility? Such advice is not included. The CIO is left in the dark.

Another feature of the advice is that no warning is included that the advice could be produced correctly yet have counterproductive results. For example, Grove's subordinates would agree that he worked hard at setting a collective mission, reassuring them that obstacles would be overcome, and that he championed the importance of intellectual stimulation. They would also agree that his leadership energy was very high. However, they also said that the actions that Grove used 'to set a collective mission', 'to reassure', and to champion 'intellectual rigorous stimulation' were counterproductive and he seemed unaware of that. They also reported that Grove championed intellectual rigorous stimulation in ways that was exhausting to them because Grove often behaved in ways that inhibited it. Finally, Grove reassured them that he was correct in defining the mission and intellectual stimulation. The problems occurred when they disagreed with his views. Grove used defensive reasoning, when, for example, he ruled out discussions of leadership styles. The subordinates, in turn used Model I actions and defensive reasoning by creating their own covert strategies for dealing with him. They covered up these strategies and covered up that they covered them up.

Bass and Riggio (2006) advise the leaders to build others' respect for them. They can accomplish this objective by acknowledging others' opinions. They are also advised not to back off from their point of view, they should avoid judging others, and should confront issues not the person (Avolio and Bass 2004).

How do leaders avoid judging others? Would Grove not assert that he seeks others' opinions? Would he not assert that he does not back off from his point of view? How can he avoid judging others when he honestly believes that it is a critical responsibility of the leader to judge others? How can he confront issues and not persons if he and others are internally committed to an issue that is part of their sense of self-esteem and self-confidence?

How can Grove or Rusk change in order to be a more effective leader with their subordinates when their subordinates use the same cover-up strategies that they themselves use? How can any of them change if they deny their personal responsibility for denying they are playing the game and that they are denying?[1]

Leadership: A Historiometric Approach

Mumford (2006) and his colleagues conduct leadership research using the historiometric approach. General conclusions are obtained by cumulating results from historic

---

[1] The research by Wu *et al.* (2007) illustrates similar problems when they use the approach to study groups.

cases and biographies. Using a careful selection device they identify 'outstanding' leaders and the crisis situation in which their leadership qualities appeared. Mumford contrasts three types of outstanding leaders. They are charismatic, ideological, and pragmatic. Mumford states that this conceptualization provides three pathways to outstanding leadership rather than the traditional one pathway of charismatic leadership.

The author's advice to produce effective leadership exhibits the same limitations of the research just cited: it is too abstract to be implemented. For example, outstanding leaders should be skilled at building intrinsic motivation. They must be effective communicators and skillful at exercising appropriate influence. They should be skillful at presenting arguments in a positive manner. Outstanding leaders do not force compliance, by seeking to shape people's personal decisions. Leaders should make integration possible. They do so by motivating, managing, and sharing directions with others. Mumford advises that leaders should be skillful at integrating their ideas with the internal environment. The advice does not specify the behavior required to produce it successfully. Moreover, it does not indicate how a leader may behave effectively if her or his actions are resisted.

I find similar questions with Zaccaro (2007). The model specifies that there are attributes (e.g. cognitive abilities, personality, motives, and values) that in turn influence such attributes as social appraisal skills, problem-solving skills, and expertise/tacit knowledge. Leaders are advised to develop their skills in dealing with cognitive complexity, cognitive flexibility, social intelligence, emotional intelligence, adaptability, and tolerance for ambiguity.

If leaders attempted to use the Zaccaro model they would find at least two problems. The list of attributes that a leader would have to develop is long. The causal connection among attributes makes the list even more complex. Second, how can a leader overcome this complexity in order to act effectively in an actual situation? Research on the human mind suggests that it is a limited information-processing system (Brown 1966; Simon 1969). A leader needs help from Zaccaro, if his model is to be actionable, specifying how to overcome the limits of the mind when acting in a real, live situation to reduce Traps.

Even if the lists are made more complete how does such clarity lead to more effectiveness? Many years ago, AT&T leadership specialists developed a blotter to be placed under the glass of senior executives' desks. This blotter advised the executives how to use concepts from the work by Neal Miller, Carl Rogers, and myself in different situations. The executives reported that trying to use the concepts, with which they agreed, immobilized them. They were immobilized not only because they did not have the skills to produce them; looking at the blotter interrupted the flow of dialogue.

Leadership: Qualitative Approaches

Bennis and his colleagues use a primary research methodology that is more qualitative in order, they suggest, to provide more opportunities to get 'closer' to understanding the respondents. The authors advise that leaders develop leadership competencies such as adaptive capacity, engaging others by creating shared meanings, voice, and integrity. Each of these features is decomposed into sub-features from which the authors derive further advice. For example, leaders should be skillful at being self-expressive and listening to their inner voice. How do leaders recognize when they are effectively listening to their inner voices? What reason do we have to think that their inner voices whisper anything other than advice based upon Model I and defensive reasoning? Rusk, Grove, and the CEOs listened to their inner voices yet acted in ways that created counterproductive consequences. Our inner voices tell us to censor ourselves, to maintain unilateral control, to win, to make topics undiscussable, and more.

The authors advise that innovative learning is key to effective leadership. How would the leaders in the cases cited above come to realize that the specific actions they use to produce innovative learning actually reinforce the status quo and inhibit innovative learning?

The authors distinguish between managers and the leaders. The managers represent a copy; the leaders are original. I find this distinction unhelpful, even odious. The problem may be that the originals act in ways to require that their managers act as if they are copies. Indeed, these originals are copies of Model I and defensive reasoning. Several years ago, Donald Schön and I participated in a week-long conference for the top management of one of our country's most respected large firms.

Professor John Kotter made a presentation on leadership. The executives rated it very highly. They publicly committed that they were going to focus more on leadership than on managership. Schön and I met with the group, after the Kotter session, for three two-hour sessions. The objective was to discuss issues that they had identified as key to the organization's performance and future. When we inquired as to what prevented them from correcting these problems, most of the participants blamed systems, routines, and lack of control. The top group behaved consistently with managership even though they said that they were committed to thinking and acting as leaders.

We raised this question at the end of the session. The senior vice president for human resources closed the session by saying that the question deserved more time. He promised to schedule it at the next yearly conference. It was not scheduled as promised. When we inquired why this did not occur, the response was that the subject was too hot and controversial to discuss with the total top group. Secretary Rusk's comment, it would be 'inappropriate', is alive and well decades later in other settings.

Magical abilities

Recently, Bennis and Thomas (2007) claimed that most leaders have at least one intense transformational experience that serves as a crucible for their transformation. Effective leaders are still seen as exhibiting four competencies, namely, adaptive capacity, engaging others by creating shared meaning, voice, and integrity. Adaptive capacity is the key competence. It is defined as almost a 'magical ability' to transcend adversity with all its attendant stresses and to emerge stronger than ever. The difficulty with the term magical as defined is that its operational meaning is a mystery. This type of mystery is maintained throughout their descriptions of the competences exhibited by those interviewed. For example:

1. They struggle in the crucibles they encounter, but they do not become stuck or defined by them.

2. They are aware not to become prisoners of their own defensive patterns to protect themselves.

3. They are not repelled by problems. They embrace them and thrive on them.

4. They are not fakes or phonies.

5. They are good at freeing themselves from others' defensiveness and then go on to unleash the potential of the other people.

6. They know how to learn.

7. They can get individuals to buy into their own version.

8. They make every 'defining moment' a basis for new ideas and new conceptions of their selves.

9. They know when and where to draw the line.

10. They can retain their youthful characteristics in adulthood.

The mysteries involved in the above include the following. What actions do they produce in order not to become stuck, not to become prisoners of their own defenses, to embrace and thrive on problems that communicates that they are not fakes, to free up themselves and others, to convince others to buy into their vision, to make 'every defining moment a basis for new ideas and new conceptions of themselves'?

Taffinder (2006) advises that effective leaders should show conviction by acting in ways that show they stand on their own, they have an opinion, display their conviction, be fervent, build relationships and trust, tell it like it is, get a regular reality check. The author does not specify how to produce these skills. Should they use Model I or Model II?

Leadership inconsistencies

Jack Welch advises that effective leaders reduce, if not destroy bureaucracies. Welch also advises freeing up employees in order to encourage sharing ideas and taking risks. Leave the employees alone to implement the advice. If they do, reward them. Treat every person with dignity. Rothschild (2007), who worked with Welch, wrote a thoughtful and positive examination of Welch's leadership behavior. His analysis supports the claims that Welch genuinely believed in implementing his ideas in a manner that showed that he treasured and nourished the voice and dignity of every person.

Rothschild then describes Welch's leadership actions as openly challenging, criticizing, and embarrassing people if he believed that doing so would motivate them. Rothschild quotes an observer of Welch's leadership that he once engaged a senior vice president in a prolonged shouting match, embarrassing the room full of managers, but then congratulated the vice president for standing up to him. Rothschild noted that he too had several similar encounters with Welch that illustrated Welch's inconsistencies.

Bower (2007) states that one of the most important leadership skills is to convince others that the leader's plan is the correct one. Convincing the others means that the leaders must exude confidence in the plan. Imparting confidence is especially challenging when the others have doubts about the leader's plan and when the others believe that their plans are better than the leader's.

How does one produce 'confidence' under these conditions? As Bower states, if the leader defers too much to the team, he or she may lose the ability to lead. If the leader demands too much deference the subordinates may leave or disengage and act as if they are not doing so. They may develop deferential habits, hold the leaders responsible, and act as if none of this is going on.

Rusk deferred too much and Grove demanded too strongly. How would Rusk test whether he is deferring too much or Grove when he is demanding too much, when the dialogue required to make such assessments is not discussable and its undiscussability is undiscussable.

Moreover, Bower's claim that one of the most important leadership skills is the ability to convince others of the leader's plan is straight Model I reasoning: it is important for the leader above all to win, not lose. Certainly, a leader with an inadequate plan should be open to learning that. The *really* critical leadership skill is the ability to work with the leadership team to produce the best possible plan and this requires Model II actions and a productive reasoning mind-set.

Becoming a Conflict Competent Leader

Runde and Flanagan (2007) advise that dealing effectively with conflict is key to successful leadership. Conflict involves uncomfortable emotions and threatening relationships. It is unlikely conflict will ever be eliminated because people have differences in values, goals, principles, and tactics. Conflict often leads to fight-or-flight types of responses. Most people react in ways that are counterproductive. They blame others. They do not seek to discover their own personal causal contributions to conflict. They deny these responses and they deny that they deny.

Runde and Flanagan's description about conflict's counterproductive consequences and my description of Traps overlap significantly. We agree that this topic is key to leadership effectiveness. The authors identify differences as a key element in conflict. They cite the preferences individuals exhibit, differences in the way they focus attention, acquire information, develop orientation, and make decisions. They cite the Myers-Briggs Type Indicator as an example of how leaders often judge these differences. The leader's ways are correct, the others are wrong.

The authors advise leaders that there are no right or wrong preferences. Effective leaders acknowledge and respect other's preferences. They seek ways to communicate them effectively. They value differences. They make sure that others in the organization do, too. Once the differences are genuinely valued, it becomes easier to overcome the frustrations of and find the strength inherent in having a diversity of preferences. Constructive responses to conflict, continue the authors, include genuinely listening to others, taking the time to understand where the person is coming from, and clarifying misunderstandings. Effective leaders seek solutions to revolving problems as opposed to looking for someone to blame.

This advice is all well and good as far as it goes. Yet unless leaders make Model II and productive reasoning their theory-in-use, it is unlikely that they will be able to go beyond paying lip service to it. Several years ago, my colleagues and I were asked to implement a two-day conference with the top executives of a very large bank. Each executive completed a left-hand–right-hand case. The executives had previously completed a two-day conference based on the Myers-Briggs. They rated the learning experience very highly. The executives claimed that they had learned to value differences in styles and to respect these differences. They now felt more understanding of the styles that differed from theirs. They publicly promised each other that they would strive to deal more constructively with the differences.

Our seminar was scheduled several months after the Myers-Briggs seminar. Ours was also rated very highly.

All the left-hand–right-hand cases that the executives completed were about business and human problems that they sought to resolve. The majority of the cases included differences in the styles that they used to understand and to make decisions. The left-hand and right-hand column data provided much evidence that the differences in views, frustrations, blaming others, were central to the problems. Yet, the executives who evaluated the Myers-Briggs conference very highly and who promised each other to respect differences showed no such respect. The MBTI seminar had done nothing to allow them to break free of the Traps produced by their Model I theory-in-action and defensive mind-set.

Narcissistic Leaders and Other Personality Types

In our analysis of Zaccaro's advice, we concluded that it was not actionable because it did not make the distinction between espoused theory and theory-in-use. Also, it would be difficult to implement his advice because it required ignoring the information-processing limitations of the human mind.

In this section, I analyze the advice of a scholar who takes into account the limitations of the human mind. His advice specifies actual behaviors to be taken from which it is possible to infer theory-in-use and reasoning mind-set. It is also possible to show that the advice is consistent with Model I and defensive reasoning which leads to Traps.

Macoby (2007) claims that there are four personality types. They are erotic (not sexual), obsessive, narcissistic, and marketing. The dominant focus of his book is upon the narcissistic type. Macoby develops the history of the concept. He shows that his meaning of narcissistic is not limited to everyday meanings such as self-absorption, arrogant, haughty, lacks empathy, and 'thinks he is superior'.

Macoby contends that these features are also adapted by the psychiatric profession. Narcissism 'has become a linguistic garbage pail piled so high with entirely negative characteristics that it has lost its descriptive power' (2007: 39). Narcissism, as the author uses it, is not a stand-in for bad manners or rude, self-centered behavior. Any one of the personality types can be selfish, self-centered, lacking in empathy, and power hungry.

The productive narcissists' rules for effective actions include to decide for themselves what is right and the values that will underlie their actions. Narcissists do not look for approval from others, do not try particularly hard to be liked or to have many friends. Narcissists develop control by recruiting people to join their world views. Narcissists create their own guidelines of meaning, of sense of purpose.

The productive narcissists use their powers to realize the potentialities inherent in themselves. They are free and not dependent on someone who controls their power, they are guided by their own purposes and the reasoning used to make this appear to them as rational. Finally productive narcissists are dedicated to persevere in their endeavors.

Productive narcissists exhibit two categories of what they consider to be strengths. The first strength is related to the substantive positions and visions that they have about their end goals or objectives. They seek confrontation of their ideas as long as the confronter knows the issues involved thoroughly. Also the confronter should be good at using rigorous thinking, clear and tight analysis.

The second category of strength is related to their personality type. They are free from psychological constraints. They focus on what is best for them and not just what others do or think they should do. This strength however contains important inconsistencies. First, the productive narcissist may be free to be himself or herself, the situation is far different for his or her subordinates. Narcissists judge the loyalty of their subordinates by the degree to which the subordinates support their personality type. The subordinates are submissive and dependent. Yet, these are the characteristics that productive narcissists do not respect. They create what they do not respect and seem skillfully aware that they are doing so.

Macoby presents detailed advice to illustrate this conclusion. For example, he advises that subordinates of productive narcissists should focus on making their boss look good. 'Realize that your usefulness to him depends on discerning what he needs, then offering it to him in the most expedient way possible' (2007: 208). Apparently, you should keep that strategy in the left-hand column.

The author warns others that a productive narcissist will call them at all hours. Be ready for these calls and accept them. 'It's that simple: Just take and try to roll with it. Don't try to lay down some kind of law and explain you have boundaries. This will not go over big with a product-ive narcissist, who has no understanding of you and your life—it is, in the end, all about him' (Macoby 2007: 213). Look for ways to let your boss shine. Let him take credit for all your good ideas. Let him blame you for his bad ideas. Be ready to swallow some humble pie.

The advice if used by the subordinates is likely to be kept in their left-hand column. The narcissistic leader uses a Model I theory-in-use as well as defensive reasoning to protect himself. He believes this is effective leadership. Ironically his model does not encourage the same behavior by subordinates.

Appreciative Inquiry

Appreciative Inquiry (AI) is based on the premise that a fundamental weakness of the traditional approaches to changing leadership and organizations is that they use a deficit approach. They focus on complaints, negative outcomes that produce diagnoses that focus upon and reinforce the negative. The result is learned helplessness and that they are victims of the system. As a result leadership and organizations are stuck in the status quo.

Leadership and organizations are best changed by asking those involved to dream and envision what might be, to dialogue about what can be, and to construct what will be. The focus is on fresh perceptions and the acquisitions of new schemes that invite experimentation to overcome the rigidity created by organizational defensive routines.

The proponents of AI recommend that leaders develop generative metaphors that present a way of seeing something new. Barrett and Cooperrider (2007) present an example: The context was to change a hotel with a poor record of customer service into one that provided more desirable service. The authors chose a 'good' hotel located in Chicago that was comparable to the 'bad' hotel except that it was an excellent producer of high-quality service. The authors created an intervention where some key employees from the 'bad' hotel visited the 'good' hotel. The participants from the 'bad' hotel were trained to conduct AI interviews. They were instructed to describe as accurately as they could the actions that they observed in the 'good' hotel that led to its positive performance. In their interviews they bypassed the 'natural' negativity and defensive cycles by asking the employee to recall events where things went smoothly and where employees cooperated. They asked the respondents to focus on peak moments, on what they valued most, and where service was high quality.

The 'good' Chicago hotel acted as a positive, liberating metaphor. The authors show that the 'bad' hotel participants began to develop an appreciative eye. They learned how to reconfigure their hotel as a creative, productive system that became alive and vital. With the AI positive approach the defensive orientation hardly appeared. Freed from habitual cynicism and doubt, the participants from the 'bad' hotel began to construct new visions and meanings that led them to make positive changes in their hotel.

Examples of the changes that they implemented included:

1. A redesign of the bell stand and the front desk; they created a coffee club.

2. A new map of the hotel becoming a 'four star hotel'.

3. Members from different departments who previously would barely speak to one another began to develop a common language to change physical space.

4. Members made a commitment to abandon the previous scripts of cycles of vengeance.

5. They raised their levels of aspirations about getting the employees to generate more energy while at work.

6. They began to move from a divided house to a more united one.

7. They began to take on a greater sense of responsibility for initiating changes in the tasks described above.

Let us agree that the positive results did, in fact, occur. One reason for these results is that all the accomplishments described above required skills that the participants had or could easily learn. Copying a positive role model is one of the easiest things to do when it does not involve learning fundamentally new skills. The solutions were primarily single-loop because the participants did not have to change their theories-in-use and their defensive reasoning in order to achieve the results.

There were a few examples of difficult interpersonal relationships where double-loop learning would be required.

For example, the employees observed differences in ways that lower level managers were behaving. They concluded that the differences were caused by superiors of those at the lower level managers. These two senior managers were told, 'You guys need to get your heads together' (Barrett and Cooperrider 2007: 140). The superiors were appalled. They met privately. They agreed that they had to straighten out their leadership behavior or they would 'Look like fools if we don't' (ibid. 144).

Another example was that someone heard the food and beverage managers claim that the room department was holding back the hotel's progress. They were confronted. 'Excuse me; I thought I went to Chicago to stop this kind of thing... If someone has a complaint about how we are doing, he should bring it up in the open' (ibid. 141).

These examples illustrate that the employees did not use the AI 'positives' that they learned. They confronted the 'guilty' actors by 'ordering' them to stop their negative actions. The orders were crafted in a manner consistent with Model I. The reasoning that was used was defensive. They put their colleagues 'on notice' by evaluating them as violating the Chicago agreement and by questioning their commitment to positive change.[2]

---

[2] Grant and Humphries (2007) describe an intervention that they conducted in four schools where they used AI research processes to guide their interviews. They concluded that, through their evocation of 'the positives', they may have dismissed, overlooked, or suppressed 'negative' messages communicated by the respondents. They also wondered if, in using AI, 'We (researchers)... may have lost valuable opportunities: to learn something unexpected; to demonstrate our commitment to participant directed research; and to deepen trust.'

Competing Commitments

Of all the leadership research that I reviewed the research on 'competing commitments' came closest to dealing with features of Traps, especially contradictions. Kegan and Lahey (2001) have developed a framework for changing behaviors at work that overcomes some of the problems described above. They focus on inconsistencies between what individuals say and how they actually behave. They focus on the personal responsibility that individuals have in creating problems.[3]

For example, there is the language of blame. In the everyday world (of Traps), blame and denial are widespread. There is also frequent expression of frustration and helplessness. The conversations are crafted in ways that generates frustration in others. The result is a language of complaint that expresses what we can't stand. Often it leaves the speaker feeling like a whiny or cynical person. Complaints are often crafted in ways that produce feelings of shame or even guilt in others.

The authors have developed a diagnostic methodology to test for, and to unfreeze, what they call immunity to change in individuals and within groups. The methodology is based upon interviewing individuals with the purpose of obtaining information on (1) their commitment, (2) what they are doing and not doing that is keeping their stated commitment from being fully realized, (3) their

---

[3] The authors have now published a more extended review of their position (Kegan and Lahey, 2009).

competing commitment and (4) their big assumptions. The diagnosis leads to a grid that paints a picture of the change community system.

The next step is to ask the individuals:

1. What they would like to see changed at work so that they can perform more effectively and make work more satisfying?
2. What commitments do your complaints imply?
3. What are you doing, or not doing, that is keeping your commitment from being more fully realized?
4. What big assumptions do you make that inhibit learning and changing (yourself and your group)?

These questions result in a diagnostic grid (see Table 4.1).

Completing this grid alerts the individuals to the inconsistencies between their actions and intended consequences. It also alerts them to make explicit the competing commitments which they had previously denied they were producing. It prompts them to surface the big assumptions that underlie their actions despite their denials that this is the case.

The grid makes transparent the defensive reasoning that leads to Traps. The grid also makes it difficult for people to deny their personal causal responsibility in creating features of Traps as well as the denials that they manufacture to deny that they are denying.

The authors caution that conducting these interviews is not easy. It does require individuals who are skillful at asking questions that are not easy to answer. Interviewers also have to be able to see that competing commitments are not signs of weakness but natural versions of

Table 4.1. Diagnostic grid

	Stated commitment 'I am committed to…'	What am I doing, or not doing, that is keeping stated commitment from being fully realized?	Competing commitments	Big assumptions
John	High-quality communication with my colleagues.	Sometimes I use sarcastic humor to get my point across.	I am committed to maintaining a distance from my white colleagues.	I assume I will lose my authentic connection to my racial group if I get too integrated into the mainstream.
Mary	…distributed leadership by enabling people to make decisions.	I don't delegate enough, I don't pass the necessary information to the people I distribute leadership to.	I am committed to having things go my way, being in control, ensuring the work is done to my high standards.	I assume other people will waste my time and theirs if I don't step in; I assume others aren't as smart as I am.
Bill	Being a team player…	I don't collaborate enough; I make unilateral decisions too often; I don't really take people input into account.	I am committed to being the one who gets the credit and to avoiding the frustration or conflict that comes with collaboration.	I assume no one will appreciate me if I am not seen as the source of success; I assume nothing good will come of my being frustrated or in conflict.

self-protection. Most individuals find it difficult to describe how they may unrealizingly inhibit the very dialogue they genuinely seek to produce.

Inadequacies of Current Management Research

The works of the researchers reviewed in this chapter and the next two chapters bypass the problem of reducing Traps because of the most fundamental assumptions the researchers hold about effective research.

The first assumption is that the objective of researchers is to describe reality and to test the validity of their descriptions by testing them as ruthlessly as possible. For the most part, they hesitate to take normative positions that would provide leaders with actionable knowledge about effective action that is based upon inquiries and critiques of the world as it is. To use the terms of our theory, researchers describe their universe as full of Model I actions and defensive reasoning that produce Traps and their consequences. That is just the way the world is, and they do not see their role as questioning reality as it is. They are willing to give advice as long as it is derived from their description. In other words, normative advice is acceptable if it assumes a Model I, defensive reasoning world. This practically rules out creating, at the theory-in-use level, a Model II world and productive reasoning because, as we have seen, even individuals who value a Model II world and productive reasoning are unable to produce it.

The second assumption held by researchers is that the research methods that they use are neutral. This claim does not stand up to careful scrutiny. The theory-in-use required to produce vigorous research is akin to Model I. For example, in the name of rigorous research, the researcher is in unilateral control of implementing the research methods. Also, in the name of validity, it is acceptable to hide, even to lie about, the theory-in-use rules to produce rigorous findings (Argyris 1980, 1993, 2004).

A third assumption that leads to difficulties is that as knowledge is built up it will lead to knowledge that is usable to reduce Traps. I have not read an argument of how it is possible to move from Model I to Model II, at the theory-in-use level. At a minimum, the argument should specify the researcher's view of the new universe and how to get from the present one to the new one. Whenever such attempts are made, they are at the espoused level. None of the research reviewed in this chapter and others (Argyris 1980, 1993, 2004) have specified how readers who seek to become more effective leaders can do so.

There is a fourth assumption that gets in the way of producing knowledge, at the theory-in-use level. Researchers assume that, if their knowledge is valid, it can be made actionable by practice and hard work. But those who are professionals in organizational double-loop change can attest that, without the Model II theory-in-use (or its equivalent), change is like the blind leading the blind and compounded by the fact that the blind deny they are blind. If they are, it is the fault of others in the system.

Speaking of the blind leading the blind, executives may be producing the same condition when they plan and implement change programs. They may be fooling themselves and unaware of their blindness. There is the example in the conclusion to this chapter. In the next chapter, you will read about a group of thirty-four CEOs who tried to help another executive act more effectively, in ways that made the situation worse, and they were unaware they did so.

Conclusions

The advice provided by these highly respected researchers is, at best, able to solve single-loop problems. The advice is inadequate to diagnosing and reducing Traps. The authors do not make such inadequacies transparent because they do not present theory-in-use methodologies that distinguish between Model I theory-in-use and defensive mind-set from Model II (or its equivalent) and a productive reasoning mind-set. Without such distinctions, reducing Traps is unlikely. Given the research methods described in the chapter, the executives will not be aware that they have been bypassing important problems.

For example, several years ago, I met with the top executives of one of the largest accounting firms in the United States. We designed a change program based around the participants writing a left-hand–right-hand case. On Monday morning the group began by discussing the case written by the managing partner. By Tuesday evening we had discussed eight cases. At the end of the day, the managing director asked that Wednesday's morning meeting start a half hour earlier.

The managing director began the session by pointing out that he had read all the cases. They made sense to him and discussing them was worthwhile. What troubled him was that, six months before, the firm had finished a large culture change program. The inside evaluations were highly positive. Moreover the evaluations made by an outside consulting firm were also highly positive.

The managing director said what troubled him was the objective of the culture change program was to reduce, if not solve, all the problems depicted in the seventeen cases of the executives around the table. 'What changes were made?' he asked with some degree of bewilderment and frustration.

The director responsible for the change program immediately responded. First, he reminded the managing director of the positive evaluations. Then he added, 'And you sir also rated the program very highly.' The managing director looked at the group and said 'I know I did and that's my bewilderment. How come I never realized this?' The directors seemed surprised and were largely silent.

5

Culture, Leadership, and Traps

(co-author Ian Smith)

Traps are created by individuals using Model I theory-in-use and defensive reasoning. Individuals deny that they are responsible for creating them. When pressed further, they deny that they are denying. Their stance is that they are victims of Traps and hence are unable to change them. Hence, Traps feedback to reinforce Model I theories-in-use and defensive reason. Self-fueling, self-reinforcing, circular processes are created that make it difficult to reduce Traps. The self-fueling, self-sealing processes can be interrupted if those involved are (or become) skilled at Model II theory-in-use and productive reasoning.

The literature on culture suggests that Traps and culture are phenomena that are beyond the individual level of analysis. Traps and culture can be conceptualized as 'supra' human phenomena with a causality of their own. Our claim is that this perspective is flawed. Generalizations about cultural change contain fundamental inconsistencies and gaps that can only be overcome by rejecting the claim that Traps are seemingly part of the sociological level. We argue that it is counterproductive to separate the individual from the sociological level. Indeed, without including the individual level of analysis, attempts to reduce Traps will not only fail, they will actually strengthen Traps. This, in turn, will result in inconsistencies and gaps that will strengthen the perseverance of Traps and the flawed generalizations about them.

We should like to illustrate the reasoning behind this claim by describing several patterns of responses that we identified when reviewing the literature on culture.

Productive and Counterproductive Cultures

There is a large degree of agreement among respondents, in the studies reviewed, as to the features of cultures that are productive of effective performance. For example, they report that productive cultures are characterized by following six features.

1. Seek and accept feedback that may not be favorable to ourselves.
2. Commit to continued cultural change and learning.
3. Encourage flexibility in the development and implementation of policies.
4. Reward risk-taking.
5. Encourage taking chances on people assignments.
6. Focus on strengthening of trust and cooperation.

Table 5.1. Factors inhibiting cultural change

1. Organizations are rigid and bureaucratic. They contain organizational defensive routines that inhibit learning and change.
2. Fear of getting into trouble by taking initiatives that organizational norms define as unpopular.
3. Lack of appropriate organizational rewards.
4. Human beings to resist accepting their share of the responsibility for the problem by blaming others or the system.
5. People develop a victim mentality that is encouraged by the organization defensive routines.
6. Lack of genuine and enthusiastic commitment by the top.
7. Most top executives do not have the time that is required to be persistent champions for persistent change.
8. Surprisingly many executives are concerned about harming their reputation if they take 'people' initiatives that are too risky.

Why are executives willing to live for years with a culture that they know is counterproductive *when at the same time* they can specify the qualities of what they consider to be a productive good culture? The executives blamed a set of eight factors, as shown in Table 5.1.

Items 1–5 place the blame on organizational factors. Items 6–8 place the blame on top executives. The argument seems to be that, if these factors can be reduced significantly, then it would be possible to implement a new culture. It is our position that reducing these factors will, at best, have a weak positive effect. More importantly the effect will not persevere. As we shall see below, the reason is that executives (like people in general) are programmed to create Traps regardless of the presence or absence of these eight factors. In fact, some of the eight factors are themselves the result of Traps—such as maintaining a victim mentality and blaming others or the system. At best, the eight factors are secondary inhibitions against creating and maintaining the positive culture that the executives seek. The primary inhibitions to renewing the culture are the Model I theories-in-use and the defensive reasoning mind-set that combine to create Traps.

How do we test this claim? We have designed and implemented six different seminars with the number of practitioners in each seminar ranging from twenty to over two hundred participants. One of these is especially relevant to testing the validity of our claim.

The Andy Case

Thirty-four CEOs attended a seminar intended to help them become more effective leaders. Each completed a left-hand–right-hand case and mailed it to me one week before they arrived. All the CEOs used Model I and defensive reasoning in their cases similar to the cases in Chapter 4.

During the first session the thirty-four CEOs were asked to analyze and discuss the Andy case (Argyris 2002). Andy was a COO, who lost what he believed was promised to him, namely a new CEO position. The old CEO agreed that he had made the promise. He withdrew the offer when he concluded that Andy was a top–down leader, too cocky, sometimes even arrogant, and blind to the political factors that he would have to deal with in order to succeed as the new CEO. The CEOs in the seminar were asked to help Andy overcome these problems in order for Andy not to make the same mistake with the next opportunity.

It is important to note Andy agreed with the diagnosis. He admitted to being blind. He asked the CEOs to act as his consultants in order to correct his blindness. The transcript of the actual dialogue between the class members and Andy (as role-played by the faculty member) shows that the CEOs failed to help Andy (Argyris 2002: 207–9).

CEO 1: You should show a sample force of strength. Measure their performance.

Andy: And how would this help me to overcome the error that I made?

CEO 1: Well you can then back up your decision, for example, with firing the two executives . . .

[*later*]

Andy: I think you are telling me that I screwed up . . . I agree. But (I need your help). What constructive action should I take?

[*later*]

CEO 9: Maybe you should have talked more openly.

Andy: Yes, what would I have said?

[*later*]

CEO 1: (Andy) is a very frustrating individual. He says he wants to learn, but I doubt it.

CEO 2: Andy was waiting for an answer he wanted to hear. He was not open to our advice.

FM: What did Andy say that illustrates that he was closed?

CEO 4: I am confused when he says to me that my advice is abstract.

FM: Did anyone hear someone say something like 'Andy, if I am going to help you, I need to know more about what it is that you find unhelpful about my advice.'

[*Silence. Several CEOs shake their heads indicating that they did not hear such comments.*]

We see that the executives did not ask for feedback, seeking to learn about their own behavior. Moreover they were blind to the impact of their behavior. Indeed, they exhibited some of the same interpersonal blindness that Andy agreed he had shown (Argyris 2002). We have thirty-four CEOs who failed to help Andy under the following conditions. Andy admitted his blindness and sought help from the CEOs. The CEOs were in a learning setting where the time and task pressures that they experienced in their own organization did not exist. The learning context encouraged them to take risks and especially learn from errors. The problem of risking their reputation was low because they would not work with each other once the seminar was over. The probability that they risked their job and their careers was close to non-existent. They were either at the top or they held majority ownership or both.

This case does not demonstrate that the organizational and cultural factors identified in the table do inhibit effective change. Reward systems and champions are necessary to enhance change. Reputational and career fears can inhibit change. Lack of time because of everyday pressures can inhibit the effective implementation of needed changes. It is *also* true that in the CEO seminar, where these conditions did not exist, the CEOs were *not* effective in helping Andy. Moreover, they were blind to how they caused their failure. They exhibited the same defensive mind-set that got Andy in trouble. In short, the CEOs created, in the classroom setting, a culture that was counter-productive to Andy's and to their own learning.

This suggests that, even when the top executives genuinely espouse support for cultural change, they are not able to produce the support under 'ideal' conditions. In our view the reason is that most leadership and cultural change programs do not deal explicitly with the primary cause of Traps, namely, Model I theories-in-use and defensive reasoning mind-sets. Attempts to change an organization's culture that bypass the behavior and theories-in-use of its members—particularly its executives—will end in frustration.

The reader may wonder if these results aren't caused by the actions of the faculty members or some action created by the CEOs during the seminar. I doubt the hypothesis because the CEOs submitted left-hand–right-hand cases describing their own leadership performance issues in their organizations. Their cases were scored by the faculty members several weeks before the seminar. All the cases were consistent with Model I theory-in-use and defensive reasoning (Argyris 2002). In addition, the CEOs admitted that they failed, but they blamed Andy for their failure. Such behavior is consistent with Model I defensive reasoning and Traps. According to our theory these results will persist when produced in any cultural change program that does not ask the participants to make explicit their Model I theories-in-use, their defensive reasoning, and how they use these factors to create Traps and to deny that they are doing so.

In the service of clarity I repeat the claim that is being made. Change programs to reduce Traps will be flawed and the results will be highly limited. What happened with the CEOs will be repeated. Any attempts to explain the limits of cultural change will focus on the eight factors described above. What will not be seen is that the limits of success to reduce Traps failed even when the eight factors were not causally operative.

There is one exception to the prediction that we are making: cultural change programs can be effective in diagnosing Traps. However, the difficulties will arise when people are made to implement actions based on the diagnosis.

The Royal/Dutch Shell Case

Ian Smith and I planned to conduct a study at Royal/ Dutch Shell[1] to show that, in order for the secondary causes of ineffective cultural change to be corrected so that the changes will persist, it is necessary to focus on the primary causes. Without effective change in the primary causes, we expected to show that the positive changes in the eight factors will not persevere.

[1] We appreciate receiving permission from Royal/Dutch Shell and David Varney to publish this case.

The champion of the cultural change program within the organization was Dr David Varney. He had undergone the type of leadership education using left-hand–right-hand cases to uncover discrepancies between Model I and Model II theories of action described in this book. Varney and his immediate reports stated that the leadership seminar was very helpful. A member of the European Management Team (EMT), Varney wanted to repeat the study at the next higher level (a level just below the top). Varney was committed to reducing the eight variables described above that typically inhibit lasting cultural change. Thus we had an opportunity to see if the top individual who is skilled at dealing with Traps and who is committed to overcoming other business difficulties is able to lead a cultural change whose results persist.

Unexpectedly, Varney left in the middle of the change program for a very prestigious opportunity. The individual appointed to replace him was curious about the program but ambivalent about continuing it. After several days of reflection, he decided to terminate our participation in the program.

The reason for including this case is that during the diagnostic phase of the program the participants made valid diagnoses of the Traps in their organization, including in their dialogues with each other. Even after Varney left many wanted to continue their learning. It was the level above the European Management Team in which Varney participated—the Country Chairmen and the very top management team, the Committee of Managing Directors (CMD)—who had devised the culture change program and who were espousing it most passionately. But as we will see, without help from professionals familiar with teaching the left-hand–right-hand case method, they were unable to move toward Model II because their theory-in-use was Model I, even though they espoused Model II. Thus we can show that Traps are the primary impediment to lasting cultural change.

Why Shell needed to change

Shell is and was a hugely successful company, amongst the best performers in the world. However, a number of senior managers were concerned that the traditional Shell culture, which had served the company so well in the past, might not be so appropriate in a rapidly changing business world.

Shell's 'familiar' competitors were other oil companies. Over the years this traditional club had been given the name the 'Seven Sisters'. Like sisters, there were often struggles and disagreements, but on the whole there was a common understanding of how the 'industry works'. The challenge that senior managers at Shell were now facing involved different types of competitors: competitors who played by different rules. For example, in the retail (filling station) business throughout Europe, the supermarket threat was intensifying. It began in France as companies like Carrefour began retailing gasoline at prices much lower than were being charged by the oil companies. The trend spread to the UK where companies like Tesco, Sainsbury, and Asda have immense muscle in general retailing. They had begun to use this muscle in the way that they sold gasoline, hurting Shell's retail business.

Even within the industry, traditional competitors were beginning to change their strategies. For instance, BP and Mobil had recently announced a major European partnership. An important part of their strategy was to rationalize their refining assets and to concentrate much more on trying to respond to the end consumer's (the motorist's) needs rather than relying on the traditional model (making money on the wholesale margins of supplying petroleum products in a traditionally under-supplied and 'cozy' competitive environment). Shell was being criticized, both publicly and privately, for its weak reaction to the new environment: For example:

'Shell has not grasped the nettle of European refining as others have done.'   ('Vital Lies', *Financial Times*, 10 May 1996)

'The spotlight is expected to move to Shell, which is widely seen to have been slow to deal with its refining assets.'

('Vital Lies', *Financial Times*, 29 February 1996)

'We could never have done a BP/Mobil. We looked and said we could not have done that and yet there is a patent need to be able to do that sort of thing.'

(Shell Europe Management Team member)

Furthermore, even before the entry of the supermarkets into the business, Shell's business was changing (although the need for change was hugely increased by the supermarkets' aggressive entry into the business). In the gasoline retailing sector, in particular, Shell (along with the other majors) was forward integrating by increasing its control of retail operations.

These shifts in competitive strategy were demanding that Shell develop new types of skills, and learn how to adapt to new types of circumstances.

How Shell needed to change

Managers at Shell, both senior and junior, were certain that these changing industry circumstances required change within Shell—and they had a clear idea of the change objectives that would ensure business success.

An extensive survey of senior and junior managers at Shell conducted by the management consulting company, McKinsey, resulted in several 'imperatives for change' from 'old' Shell to the 'new' Shell. We present these imperatives below along with representative statements from Shell managers. Note the similarities between these features and culture and those described at the outset of this chapter.

From a risk-averse to a *risk-taking* culture:

They have all developed a system where they wait for instructions. They all like to hear what their bosses would like them to do. The key challenge is to kill that attitude and to get people to be proactive and to use their skill.

We are afraid of taking risks and we ultimately lack, despite what some of us say some of the time, self confidence.

From diffuse responsibilities to *clear accountability*:

You could always duck responsibility. You were never able to sit down and look somebody in the eye and say 'you were responsible for that being a good result and for that not being a good result' because you could always say the bad result was somebody else's problem.

From analysis to paralysis to *acting* on 80 percent diagnoses:

We need to go for the 80/20 solution and then pick up the 20 by learning. The environment isn't going to sit and wait for us.

From a 'fat cat' to a *'lean and mean'* mentality:

We are still fat cats. Money is coming out of our ears and to change mind-sets under such circumstances is not easy.

We are living off the past. I look at the last ten years and I ask 'What have we actually done to create a future for ourselves?'

From a national to a *European outlook*:

There is a real tension between how much of my resource I should give to Europe and how much attention I should give to my own country.

You get bits of information from here and there, that the role of the OpCos (Operating Companies) will remain. This then spreads through the organization and it's deadly. One wonders how we can still go on like this.

We've operated for so long in terms of having a very strong national operating company identity with a lot of independence and if you go back a few years, the good guys or the heroes were the guys who actually defended their patch and would fight the rest of the organization, and so you have a culture which is in that mould.

From an internal to an *external focus*:

We just look inside. We love having tough discussions between ourselves—but we're losing our grasp on the market vis-à-vis our customers and suppliers. I know suppliers who are thinking 'Are these Shell people serious?'

You just wouldn't believe how much energy is spent internally on the organization.

From political behavior to *open communications*:

Shell culture is brilliant at not actually ever having confrontation about anything. We arrive at consensus through a very complicated process. I believe very strongly that in the end, the old empire we ended up with was a dishonest culture. People were not saying what they really felt on quite a massive scale.

Shell's process of change

The consensus was that Shell should develop a vision organized around concepts, which, in turn, would embody the values. Typical concepts were: 'achieving breakthrough performance'; 'encouraging ownership of business issues'; and 'being tough on meeting performance objectives':

We won't get the sort of breakthroughs we need unless we create some breakdowns. I don't mean consciously create some breakdowns but I think if you look at the individuals, I think there are blockers in place in David's (David Varney's) team.

The next step would be to change organizational configurations and reporting relationships to make them consistent with the new requirements:

The key players on the European convergence team have a boss who is often the chairman of the local operating company, and I think that puts them in an invidious position at times.

Functional groups and business groups have got to change.

Thereafter, Shell would develop new, supportive policies, such as reward and penalty systems, performance appraisals, and new leadership programs:

The reward for a successful career was the country organization and it's less clear now where the career goes, and what the career path is, and how careers are managed.

There was a sort of ritual whereby you went out and did an operating job, you came back to the center, you were sort of recycled. This was a place to hide. The psychological contract was that as long as you kept your nose clean you'd be cycled round the system from cradle to grave.

These new ideas, such as breakthrough performance, would be pursued with 'religious zeal', combined with appeals from senior managers for a sense of urgency:

We are not being radical enough in what we are doing and in my view all praise goes to David [Varney] because he is being very radical about it. He's pushing back the barriers all the time.

Shell's actual results

As documented above, there was widespread and unchallenged consensus at all levels of management about what was needed at Shell and how the change process should work, but in the end little happened. In fact, those who were most invested in the change process got stuck and were unable to move it forward. How and why did this happen? There were three ways in which the various management factions seemed to get 'stuck':

1. There was poor dialogue between the top (the Country Chairmen) and the very top management team (the Committee of Managing Directors—the CMD) on the one hand and the next level, Shell Europe Management Team. In interviews with Europe Management Team members there was an evident lack of trust in what their bosses were doing.

2. There was frustration within the Shell European Management Team about the ability of their own group to come to grips with the tough business issues that the company was facing.

3. More junior, but high-potential managers who were given voice in the Joint Force group, which was specifically created to help the 'Young Turks' in the organization push for change, felt increasing frustration at the slow pace of change.

We describe below the ways in which managers at these three levels got stuck, and how this 'stuckness' demonstrates ways in which these managers were preventing cultural change at the very moment that they were swearing allegiance to the need for change.

How the top of the organization got stuck

As noted, it was the top two levels of the organization (the Country Chairmen and the CMD) who had devised the culture change program and who were espousing it most passionately. Their espousal often became so passionate that it would be more accurate to say that they were pleading with the rest of the organization to change. The exhortations from the top suggested a lack of trust in the commitment to change lower down the organization. In fact, what the European Management Team (the next level down) needed was not cajoling, but real faith that the top level was serious about its commitment for change, and had confidence in the European Management Team's ability and willingness to effect it.

The Top Management had structured the European Management Team with ambiguous powers and responsibilities, which the European Management Team read as a compromise (and hence an 'Old Shell' action) between the new values of urgency and responsibility on the one hand and the old 'baronial' culture on the other. As one manager put it, 'The big problem that the CMD identified subsequently of muddied responsibilities and conflict was one they had introduced themselves.' This had two consequences: First, it lessened the EMT's faith in the top's commitment to change. Second, it created an immobilized and impotent EMT that looked to David Varney, their leader, to act. In other words all members of the team, except David Varney, began sliding back into Old Shell ways.

The Shell Europe Management Team got stuck

For their part, EMT avoided discussing the ambiguity of their role and responsibilities. They blamed Top

Management for creating ambiguity, but failed to confront them with it. 'For my part there was a passive acceptance that some good will come out of this process and therefore it was pretty futile and almost destructive to challenge it', one said. And they avoided talking about their impotence: 'We all discussed refinery closure, while we all knew that there was nothing we could do about it.'

They espoused risk-taking, but sought their bosses' 'sign-off' and approval for actions. As one manager put it, 'Yes I would like my cake and eat it. I will take a risk if you indemnify me in advance.'

Within EMT discussions the group displayed high advocacy ('I'm right, you're wrong'), low additivity (ignoring what was said by the person before, and advocating a completely new position on a completely new topic), low integration (not saying 'if I put that view/data together within mine, then you would conclude that . . . '). That is, they would each express a strong opinion. That option would not be linked to the previous comment. No one took any responsibility for pulling things together (although the chairperson vainly tried to summarize things at the end of the meetings), so the discussion ended with a babble of opposing views, all presented as discrete statements. No trade-offs were made, and no conclusions were reached. In other words, these high-echelon managers behaved very much like the young MBA students in the case presented earlier. And this unhelpful behavior was almost totally related to the 'easy' issues. The more difficult business problems were not even discussed at all. As one EMT member put it, 'The easy solutions are dealt with by the committee, the EMT: the difficult ones are dealt with by the network.'

The level of dysfunction was highlighted by a 'Green Paper', written by David Varney, that tried to clarify the structure that would make the European Management Team work. Although it represented an intense power struggle between Varney and the 'Barons', the political implications of the paper—although avidly discussed in private—were meticulously avoided in public discussion. 'We are all polite', one manager said. 'We know what the constraints are, we can think ourselves into the Shell position. But of course we didn't say this openly.'

There was very little reflectiveness about the barriers to change. For example, the EMT held a discussion about a roof-coating product which the organization had failed to roll out across Europe. It was generally agreed that this was very irritating, since it had been attempted numerous times before. But no one asked the question: what is it about the way we do things that prevents a European roll-out despite it having been discussed many times before? And why can't we ask ourselves this type of question?

The EMT also backtracked in dealing with their subordinates. Despite the new values, which advocated holding subordinates accountable for business logic, the actual behavior within meetings was often soft on sloppy thinking. For example, there was a proposal to split the Benelux region between France and Germany, but without any business justification. This was noted by the EMT but they did not ask why the business unit felt they could present a proposal to them that had no business justification.

How the 'Joint Force' got stuck

As noted, young high-potentials or 'Young Turks' were brought together into a Joint Force to help push for change. The 'Young Turks' argued the case for change with forceful rhetoric, but they demonstrated, underneath the words, a strong alignment with the very culture that they were denigrating. Their rhetoric, for instance, contained no ideas about how words might be turned into action. Another example: they placed blame for inaction on the level above them, rather than reflecting on their own responsibility for the lack of change.

The Joint Force members were creating the very environment that they despised:

- They called for more individual responsibility, but ended up by blaming others.
- They denounced bureaucracy, but ended up by calling for the creation of even more committees to '*bring about change*'.
- They called for openness and a real dialogue, but they ended up by suggesting the removal of anyone opposing them.

What went wrong: a diagnosis

Shell is a highly successful and profitable organization. It would be very unlikely, therefore, for the organization to get things wrong all of the time. We believe that it was only within the context of certain critical issues that Shell was becoming stuck, primarily because of a lack of appropriate conceptual tools to overcome the problems.

We believe this because we noticed that when we confronted people about their own responsibilities toward their team's 'stuckness', they mostly responded non-defensively, and seemed able to frame issues in a different way. That is, Shell people displayed high levels of commitment, of openness to learning, and of intellectual integrity. Why is it then that, with the very best of intentions and a high level of commitment to sustainable change, the Shell Europe Management Team and its members still found themselves stuck as described above? The data (interviews with managers throughout the organization, and tape recordings of what actually goes on in meetings) suggest a number of possible hypotheses.

THE CONSENSUS FOR CHANGE WAS COUNTERFEIT

The logic here might be that conservatism was deeply embedded within the organization, and that, whatever was said publicly, people were resistant to change or lacked passion and urgency to change. Supporting this view, one manager told us, 'People don't actually believe that a performance culture is necessary.'

PEOPLE LACKED TRUST IN TOP MANAGEMENT

Perhaps people were untrusting of the genuine desire for change by the top management, and hence would consider unquestioning enthusiasm for real change as personally risky (while, at the same time, publicly 'saluting' calls for change). 'Too many people in Shell believe Van

Wachem (the personification of the "old guard") will win', one manager said.

PEOPLE HAD A PERSONAL STAKE IN THE 'OLD' SHELL

A third possibility is that there were genuine conflicts of interest in that some people had a real stake in the status quo. 'We're not getting everybody on board because at some stage in these changes there will be losers', one person said. 'Some people will only lose, and it's a fairytale to hope you can ever get them on board.'

But our contact with both senior and junior managers suggested that most people *were* genuinely committed to the New Shell. Perhaps there are other explanations.

CHANGE JUST TAKES A LONG TIME IN A BIG ORGANIZATION

'Bringing about change in an organization like Shell takes a long time' was a typical comment. 'It's like turning around a giant oil tanker. You've just got to be patient and careful if you want it to succeed.' But the same problems keep coming up. Sustainable change seems elusive.

THE PROBLEM IS DIFFICULT INDIVIDUALS, WHO NEED TO BE ROOTED OUT AND GOT RID

As one manager said, 'The problem we have is those so-called barons, who don't want to lose their playgrounds.' But there was no agreement on what the profile of a difficult person would be, and what would stop new barons appearing. If this is an accurate explanation for what has gone wrong in the past, then it will be a fair prediction of what will go wrong in the future. Still, the process of changes will not move forward.

There is an element of truth in all of the above diagnoses as to why it seems so difficult to implement change. But they leave too much unexplained. This led us to believe there is a more fundamental diagnosis: *It is that the 'how to get there'—Shell's theory of change—is not sufficiently actionable.*

The Shell theory of change

Summarizing the observations above, the Shell theory of change has the following elements:

- It identifies a vision and values such as 'breakthrough performance' and 'ownership'.
- It tries to remove structural ambiguities about lines of reporting responsibility.
- It advocates change in culture and behavior.
- The end of 'Shell speaks'.
- More risk-taking.
- It brings reward and appraisal systems into line with the new values/vision.

All of these initiatives need to be undertaken with

- exhortation;
- calls for urgency;
- clear signs of commitment from the top;
- coaching from the top.

But, things did not change. Why not?

The change process beset by Traps

The data suggested to us that when barriers to change were encountered, there did not seem to be any capacity to reflect and address the gap between what Shell people set out to do (their espoused theory) and the reality of the way that people behaved (their 'theory-in-use'). *The Shell theory of change is incapable of explaining those situations where it breaks down.* Therefore, when new behaviors were really needed (really mattered because the issues were important) this was exactly the time when the old behaviors would dominate. If our theory was correct, then it would explain a number of things that we had been observing when the organization seemed to get 'stuck'.

In fact, when the data are examined, a pattern emerges. There are a number of business issues which Shell handles efficiently and with despatch. On the other hand, there are a number of issues, with systematic characteristics, that the organization seems to be unable to deal with effectively. The two categories—easy and difficult—are shown in Table 5.2.

When the 'difficult' types of issues were on the table, there were recurrent patterns of behavior:

- a very strong espoused commitment to the 'New' Shell but an inability to create it;
- a self-defeating reversion to 'Old' Shell behaviors at critical moments;

Table 5.2. How conventional approaches bypass traps

Relatively easy	Very difficult
Simple e.g. investment in cat cracker	Complex e.g. potential for zone to contribute to the 'supermarket' problem
Easy implementation e.g. smart card launch in UK	Complicated implementation e.g. implementing European refinery rationalization
Consistent with traditional lines of organization and power e.g. Service company rationalization	Cuts across traditional lines of organizational power e.g. the *final* decision on commonback office
Low level of 'integration' e.g. ARB	High levels of 'integration' e.g. pan European joint (MST)
Expansion and 'colonization' e.g. replicating OpCo structure in new markets	Marketing initiatives Contraction and prioritization e.g. investment in Russia and Eastern Europe

- a 'skilled unawareness' of this bind;
- a tendency to avoid embarrassment and threat, to avoid conflict, and to blame others (publicly);
- a lack of public (i.e. in meetings of more than two Shell people together) discussion of the problem;
- the undiscussability of the lack of public discussion.

As we have seen, all of these characteristics are manifested in Traps: skilled unawareness, blaming others, making things undiscussable, and making the undiscussability itself taboo. In other words, Shell's managers espoused the New Shell values, but reverted to old behaviors in the interests of expediency. One EMT member, a passionate exponent of the need to move to the New Shell values, described how he had used a very political process, a typical set of Shell moves, in order to get an action implemented. When confronted with the view that such behavior would ensure that the Old Shell values would persist, the manager replied, 'But that is the only way you can get things done around here.'

This was not an isolated incident; behaviors often reverted to Old Shell values. Table 5.3 'scores' the quality of dialogue in a series of Shell Europe Management Team meetings. Down the left-hand side are the issues that required decision and action. Along the top are the new values that this senior team wanted to see acted out in the 'New Shell culture'. From the tapes of the meetings, and from real-time interventions, we scored the way in which the EMT members acted out the new values. For example an 'X' in the column means that when the management team was discussing a decision on bitumen, then they shied away from establishing greater personal accountability (by missing the opportunity to alert their subordinates that the business logic for merging territories was weak), thus 'betraying' that value.

Whenever EMT members described how they would actually go about doing something, they reverted to the 'Old' Shell ways and were either

- unaware of the reversion, or
- justified it in terms of 'but we have to compromise this time, it's important, and it's the only way to get it done'.

This pattern of behavior has dangerous consequences for the change process. First, subordinates, who are perfectly

Table 5.3. Old versus new values

Issues	Addressing tough issues	Risk-taking	Greater personal accountability	Action based on 80/20 analysis	External focus	Clear & honest communication	Unambiguous messages	Rigorous thinking
Bitumen	X		X		X	X	X	X
Green Paper	X	X	X		X	X	X	X
Relationship with top	X	X	X		X	X	X	X
Relationship with each other	X	X	X		X	X	X	X
Relationship with subordinates	X	X	X		X	X	X	
Refinery rationalization	X	X	X	X	X	X	X	X
Supermarket threat	X	X	X		X		X	X
BP/Mobil deal		X	X	X	X		X	X

X = New Shell value betrayed.

alert to the hypocrisy, will continue to be socialized and acculturated with the 'old' values. Secondly, it will not achieve its objectives, such as 'breakthrough performance' and 'open and honest behaviour', because people will be, in actuality, behaving in the old, dysfunctional ways. This will inevitably provoke cynicism. As one manager commented: 'The reorganization process has been a total disaster. If the right opportunity came up I would leave.' Another said, 'People don't see the substance behind it. They see a lot of evangelical fervour but what does it actually mean? We see words like "breakthrough performance" but what does that mean? What is the plan to deliver it?'

In spite of all this, or perhaps because it of it, there was a tendency to shield subordinates from ambiguity, despite the 'new' value that espoused honesty, openness, and personal responsibility. One manager justified that by saying, 'They have to believe there's a God up there sometimes. How much uncertainty do you share? If you're a refinery operator and you see that the Gods have feet of clay, that's not very rewarding.'

Reflecting on Cultures and Traps

Schein (1992, 1999) defines culture as having three levels. They are artifacts (visible organizational structures and processes), espoused values (strategies, goals, philosophies), and basic underlying assumptions (unconscious, taken-for-granted beliefs, perceptions, thoughts, and feelings).

Sackman (1991) defines culture as a set of commonly held cognitions that are held with some *emotional investment* and integrated into a logical system or cognitive map that contains cognitions about *descriptions, operations, prescriptions*, and *causes*. They are *habitually used* and influence prescription, thinking, feeling, and acting.

Both authors agree that the components of culture become attached to emotion and degrees of importance. The components are relatively stable over time. This provides a sense of order and makes the world predictable. Schein and Sackman suggest that culture is used to answer characteristic questions, such as 'what is', 'what exists', 'how are things done' or 'should be done', and 'why things are done the way they are' (Sackman 1991: 39).

Fundamental differences between cultures and Traps

Both authors pay considerable attention to specifying these features in more detail. Whatever their respective details, both authors hold that the components form patterns of interdependence that result in the patterns being self-fueling and self-maintaining. The patterns also develop over time as well as in the context in which they exist. Cultures are complex. Variance is a key feature of all cultures.

The structure and processes cannot be defined ahead of time without deep understanding of their content. We may know that cultures are composed of artifacts, espoused values, and underlying assumptions. But they cannot be defined a priori. We also know that the components are embedded with emotional investment, specify causes, and are habitually used.

Unlike culture, Traps are the same over time and in different contexts. The primary causes of Traps are the use of Model I theory-in-use and the defensive reasoning mind-set. All Traps are characterized by denying personal causal responsibility, and covering up the denial by making it undiscussable.

And Traps universally inhibit learning to correct the counterproductive consequences they create. As we saw in the cases presented in Chapter 2, Traps are activated regardless of whether the subject matter is intentions or technical problems. We have also illustrated how teaching that can detect and correct errors can be blocked by individuals, groups, and organizational norms such as defensive routines.

The literature on culture claims that culture can develop from bottom–up or top–down. Most writers seem to focus on the ways the top executives create and influence culture. It is true that top managements do influence the conditions under which Traps are activated and the degree to which they are protected by the top. Using this criterion, it follows that the top is more influential. But, if the criterion to be used is how human beings learn to be skillful at creating and maintaining Traps, then all begin with similar Model I skills and defensive reasoning mind-sets. Most individuals, regardless of sex, age, education, or wealth, learn Model I and defensive reasoning through acculturation. They *enter* organizations skilled at creating Traps and accept Traps as 'natural'.

Leaders who create Traps by their top–down actions and policies are matched by the subordinates creating their own Traps. The difference is that in most cases the subordinates drive their actions underground. They design and execute them with skilled transparency. We saw this with Shell, where the top levels of the organization created Traps and the 'Young Turks' responded by constructing their own.

As noted, the executives in the EMT displayed high advocacy and intransigence, low additivity, and low integration (not saying 'if I put that view/data together within mine, then you would conclude that . . . '). In the case of the MBAs we discussed in Chapter 2, they created Traps that were counterproductive to effective dialogue about compensation strategies in a classroom exercise. At Shell, discussions about making real changes in a multibillion dollar international enterprise ended with a similar babble of opposing views, and no conclusions were reached.

The primary source of Traps is not culture

To promote open and honest communication, risk-taking, and other productive values, many consultants and executives focus on the organization's culture. But as the Shell case demonstrates, the culture is a by-product of the behavior of the people in the organization. The primary sources of Traps are the inner contradictions created by the skillful use of Model I and defensive reasoning. The players act out their Traps in groups, in interpersonal relations, in organizational defensive routines, and in the underground world—all of which will be reflected in the organization's culture.

Given all the built-in protective actions and defensive reasoning in Traps, they cannot be diagnosed effectively by using espoused theory data. In order to diagnose Traps it is necessary to begin with relatively observable data such as tape-recordings of actual meetings and conversations or observations by highly skilled observers. The caution by Schein against depending upon surveys is valid not so much because we do not know what to ask. Indeed, Trap theory specifies the variables ahead of time. The problem with surveys is that they start with respondents' beliefs and claims, by using espoused theory data. The theory-in-use that activates Traps is not the same theory that respondents refer to in filling out surveys.

When it comes to change on the organizational or personal level, the key criterion for success is the development of Model II action and productive reasoning skills. Traps can be reduced significantly by educating individuals to use Model II theory-in-use and productive reasoning. The training depends on practice under everyday life conditions. Learning Model II and productive reasoning can be used for both technical and interpersonal types of knowledge. This is the basis for genuine integration of the technical and people issues in organizations.

A focus on change to increase effectiveness in the marketplace, in order to become operational, will have to focus on learning. For example, Want (2006) recommends changing addictive cultures. He specifies that education is the first step to getting rid of addictions. The second step is to replace old constraints with more functional ones. The third step is consensus building. The final step is action. In order to make this advice actionable, it is necessary to specify the steps in educating, in replacing, in creating consensus, and in taking action. The context of these steps is significantly different depending on the theory-in-use and the reasoning mind-set used. If we focus on espoused theories, as most culture change programs do, we will meet frustration, as happened at Shell.

6

Strengthening New Approaches

We have seen how neither leadership nor culture by themselves can reduce or eliminate Traps. Of course, prescriptions to create new levels of performance in organizations are not limited to these two topics. New approaches to strengthen organizations and their management abound as consultants and scholars steadily present new practices and theories. These approaches ask us to address organizational performance on the basis of the psychological well-being of its members, strengthening teamwork, promoting organizational learning, improving collaboration, ensuring strategic fit, and other strategies. A few of these new approaches address the existence of Traps in one form or another, but many seem unaware of the existence of Traps, or simply bypass them. As I will show in this chapter, each can in fact be strengthened by including features of our approach in order to reduce Traps.

Before turning to these new approaches, however, I should acknowledge that many of those in large organizations seem to find the existence of Traps unremarkable: supposedly 'savvy' managers acknowledge Model I defensive reasoning as a fact of life and simply make use of it for their own purposes. For example, a large corporation recently promoted some individuals as stars. They went through a carefully designed set of seminars to introduce them to the values of the organizations as well as to the leadership skills valued by the organization. The person in charge of these educational seminars was a highly trusted HR executive personally selected by the CEO. At the end of each of the seminars, the HR executive held a session with the young executives. He promised to be 'brutally' honest and asked for a commitment from the executives to keep the session confidential.

In one seminar, the executives had recently observed a session between the CEO and his reports. The idea was to help the young executives to see the top in action dealing with the topics of investments and innovation. The HR executive reminded the new executives that the CEO's immediate reports rank-ordered five investment alternatives. The session ended with numbers 2 and 3 being selected. The HR executive asked the young executives, in this session, to describe their reactions to the top executives' discussion. Those who spoke, and they represented the majority, described the session as open, frank, and involving.

The HR executive then told the young executives that he attended a session of the CEO's immediate reports in preparation for their meeting with the CEO. The immediate reports expressed concern that the CEO might bypass or not approve their preferred alternatives, so they designed a strategy. The lead presenter would present alternatives 1 through 3 as 'throw-aways' or tests. These alternatives were designed to uncover clues about the likely position of the CEO. The direct reports specified criteria that, if observed, would mean that they should omit the two most important recommendations and cover up that they were doing so. At the meeting, the lead presenter ended the meeting after the first three options were presented because his reading of the clues told him they needed to delay discussion of options 4 and 5 until after they softened up the CEO.

The young executives were taken aback. What about all the pleading for openness and candor, they asked? The HR executive responded that these values were still respected but not at the expense of options 4 and 5. Several of the young executives expressed admiration for the skill of the executives in hiding their strategy and acting as if they were not doing so. The HR executive said, in effect, that this was the most important lesson for the young executive. He advised them to develop such skills.

Imagine that this type of dialogue occurs over the years. Imagine also the numbers of 'confidential' sessions the younger executives may hold to teach their subordinates how to survive. How many games must be played and how undiscussable those games must be! It is against this sort of environment that many of today's experts and researchers advance their approaches to organizations: promoting teamwork, trust, collaboration, and so on. It may be unfair to call them naïve, yet we must point out that those who overlook the power and ubiquity of Traps will find their prescriptions for change continuously undermined.

Seeking Help from Outside Consultants

Some, acknowledging the pervasiveness of Traps and the difficulties of dealing openly with them—and perhaps adopting the defensive reasoning mind-set that 'we are all victims'—seek help in the form of an intervention from outside the organization. While not new, the use of consultants is one of the most common organizational fixes—and the solutions the consultants offer are frequently touted as 'new and improved'. Organizations bring in consulting teams, often from prestigious firms, to diagnose their troubles and offer prescriptions for change. Since these consultants are outsiders and professionals, they are expected not to be burdened with the baggage that organizational members carry and to use productive reasoning rather than a defensive mind-set in their dealings with clients. Unfortunately, these expectations are often unmet.

I should like to describe the difficulties that I have witnessed in consultants' interactions with clients when productive reasoning has been used in the service of Model I. The consultants with whom I have worked tend to evaluate their professional skills very highly. They reported that they are not in the business of bragging publicly (in their groups or in groups with clients). Yet, as a senior executive in one consulting firm said, during a meeting with the top consulting group, 'When we ask, "mirror, mirror on the wall who is the fairest person of them all" the answer is me' (Laughter).

I asked twenty-four highly senior consultants if they had occasions when they believed that they had delivered an excellent report yet the clients expressed doubts. All said yes, and all said that it was not often. I then asked them how they responded. All answered that they wanted to understand the reasoning behind the client's evaluations. The strategies that they reported they used included:

1. Welcome the client's questions and concerns. Do so in a manner that the discussions are based on objective facts and not upon ideologies.

2. Review the main points of our analysis and recommendations to make certain that the clients understand our reasoning and our positions.

3. If emotions rise, calm the people down by examining rationally how they developed their assessments of our work.

These responses are consistent with productive reasoning. For example, focus on the objective facts and not upon ideologies. Make sure that the clients realize the rigorousness of our thinking, especially our willingness to subject our substantive claims to as robust tests as we and the clients can generate. Calm any emotions down by focusing upon our reasoning and upon the facts.

To the degree that these strategies reflect aspects of Model II reasoning, they should be less likely to produce

Traps. However, there is still some danger here, depending on how the consultants actually produce these strategies. An examination of the left-hand columns of the consultants revealed a number of theories-in-use that could make these conversations less effective. For instance, (a) it is important that we understand each other; (b) make sure that the clients really understand us; (c) help the clients to craft their views as rigorously as possible, and test their views but (d) do all this without offending the client, (e) do not arouse strong emotions and (f) if emotions arise, dampen them by focusing on the clients' reasoning, not their emotions. If the consultant reminds the client that ideologies must be excluded, the client may respond (probably in their head) 'I know that perfectly well. I think it's you who are having trouble parting with your own ideology.' If the consultant says, 'Let's make sure to separate emotions from facts', the client may think (but not say) 'I'm not emotional, but they seem to be getting emotional. If they are getting emotional, they might have trouble seeing how our position is valid. And for the record, I am focusing on the correct facts, namely my facts.'

We see additional recipes for introducing Traps with clients when we look at the strategies that consultants use in managing clients. They are (a) set clear tasks for the clients who are on the joint team charged with making the analysis and developing the recommendations; (b) keep the pressure on them, don't let them off the hook; (c) do the work for them so that progress is not inhibited; (d) warn the clients that the tools are sophisticated, make public our warning labels, that the tools can be detrimental to performance if not used correctly.

These strategies are consistent with Model I. The consultants are unilaterally controlling. They act to protect the clients from possible failure by maintaining tougher control over the clients' actions. They acknowledge that they may be more Model I and use stronger defensive reasoning in order to protect themselves. They may espouse Model II actions but believe that such a dialogue may upset the clients. I should like to turn to several examples to illustrate the problem.

Case A

The clients had conducted their own internal analysis of a new venture. They concluded that the new venture could become a billion dollar plus business. The consulting team was asked to help the clients position themselves to take advantage of the opportunity. The team worked cooperatively with the client organization. After several months of work and periodic lengthy discussions, the consulting case team presented to the client their analysis. They concluded that it was unlikely that the business would be more than a seventy-five million dollar one (at least in the immediate future). As the senior consultant officer stated, 'We became aware that there was a lot of nit-picking of analytical points. For the first time we were asked questions by the clients such as, "When did you get that number?" or, "How do you know that your assumptions are correct?"'

The senior consultant officer then asked his consultants how they would diagnose what was going on. The consultants responded that the nit-picking was caused by the clients' defensiveness. 'What would make the clients defensive?' asked the officer.

The consultants responded to the officer's questions with three reasons. First, the consultants had produced more pessimistic conclusions than the clients had expected. The nit-picking was caused by feelings of embarrassment by the client. Second, the consultants had not only told the client that their projections were wrong. They also created the possibility that at least some of the client's people brought in to build the new business might lose their jobs. Third, the surprise itself could be a cause of the client defensiveness. If the consultants had spoken with some of the key individuals before the meeting, they could have prepared them for the surprise.

As one consultant said, 'Their nit-picking is a survival process to be expected by anyone who is threatened' (many nodded their heads approvingly or said 'Yes', 'Correct', 'Right on'). He added, 'Would we not act in the same way if we had an outsider tell us that our analysis was wrong?' Again, many nodded their heads approvingly and several said 'Yes'. We have an example where the consultants agreed that the clients were acting defensively. They also admitted that they would do the same if their work was threatened.

The officer leading the discussion asked how the consultants should respond. Their responses included (a) ask the clients to 'raise their sights . . . and help them to see the big picture'; (*b*) encourage the clients to examine 'our numbers any way they wish and see what happens to the analysis. If we are correct they will eventually realize it'; (*c*) invite the clients to express all their views—'we then promise to think about them and promise to respond. In the meantime, let us get on with the presentation'; and (*d*) begin the presentation with more positive findings and then ease into the negative conclusions.

All these strategies assume that clients who are feeling defensive have the capacity to reduce their defensiveness either by asking them 'to raise their sights' or by beginning with some positive examples. It is as if human beings can distance themselves from their own defensive reasoning actions and then continue to focus dispassionately on the data that are causing the threat in the first place. There is also a plea to suppress the defensiveness in order to overcome it. The clients are expected to place their defensiveness 'on hold' and discuss threatening subjects with dispassion. These strategies are being recommended even though earlier many of the consultants had agreed that they too would have reacted defensively if someone had told them something that was equally surprising about their practice, using their data to make the point.

During the discussion, consultant A said that he would have asked the client, 'to temporarily suspend disbelief, to focus less on the details, and more on the major pieces of the analyses'. Consultant B responded, 'But that would be adding insult to injury. Moreover, the clients could experience A as acting in a patronizing manner.' There were few moments of awkward silence since this was the first time one of the consultants had negatively evaluated the contributions of another consultant.

The officer asked A how he felt about B's response. A said that he felt B had not understood him. The officer then asked, 'If the conversation continued as it did, would you have felt B and others would be nit-picking?'

A responded, 'Yes'. The officer then pointed out that A had concluded that his colleagues were wrong and acted as if that was not the case. A continued to hold his views strongly while discounting the views of his critics. B smiled when he heard A's comments and said: 'To be honest, and I guess that's the idea of these sessions, I would have probably reacted the same way as A did.'

The moment the threat occurred in their own discussion, the consultants also acted in ways to bypass potential threat and to distance themselves from it. These defensive strategies made it unlikely that the consultants would test publicly their own attributions about defensiveness or obtain the cooperation they seek from the clients to overcome theirs.

Case B

A consulting team had as its objective to collect valid financial data. They met with fifteen key client middle managers (line/staff). They were unable to get from them relatively clear and unambiguous answers about the meaning of the numbers. After many hours of frustration, they scheduled individual meetings in an attempt to get clearer answers, but met with little success. When the consultants were alone, they made comments such as 'unbelievable', 'They're all screwed up', 'Have you ever seen such a defensive group?', 'No wonder the top management does not trust the planning process.'

The team leader admonished the members to deal 'sensitively with the client members because they and the organization were obviously defensive' and 'we don't want to get mired down in their organizational garbage'.

Let's look at what actually happened here. The consulting team members observed the reactions of the line and staff managers to their questions. The team members concluded that the clients and the client system were acting defensively. The intended attribution of defensiveness became the premise for guiding the team's actions. The team members' design for dealing with the clients included such strategies as (1) do not discuss the defensiveness in order to test or understand it because (2) that will most likely make the clients more defensive and (3) act as if the clients are not judged as being defensive, therefore (4) cover up the diagnosis with a bypass strategy. These rules are consistent with Model I and defensive reasoning.

There are several important consequences of this strategy. First, the consultants may not learn the extent to which their diagnosis may have been incorrect. Second, the clients may not learn the extent to which their defensiveness inhibits the formulation, development, and execution of a strategy. Third, if the clients react defensively, and if the consultants bypass that defensiveness, then the consultants have introduced into the client organization routines for dealing with defensiveness designed to bypass the defensiveness and act as if this is not being done. The result is a cover-up and further reinforcement of the Traps. Some may say that the consultants would not have gotten themselves in such a predicament if they had involved the clients more in the process. But, the example came from a meeting where the team and the clients were working cooperatively from the outset.

The client organization is not being helped to understand that its defensive routines inhibit it from learning how to learn. One consequence of this is related to the reactions of the executives at the top. They created the case team (an internal task force with outside consultants) precisely because they did not believe that the present organization could produce the analysis necessary for a sound strategy. They reached that conclusion after several years of experience with their own planning process that resulted in all sorts of incomplete or incorrect plans which the top concluded were the result of the defensiveness of the organization. Like everyone else involved in this case, the top executives also kept their diagnosis secret. They too covered up, they too covered up the cover-up, and they too bypassed the entire issue by hiring the outside consultants to work with the 'best' individuals that they could identify from within the organization.

To sum up: the automatic reaction to defensiveness in both cases is to ignore or bypass the defensiveness. But the act of ignoring reality is itself defensive because individuals who are charged with producing a new strategy eventually will have to deal with the existing organizational defensive routines because they will operate to reduce the effectiveness of the new planning processes. Bypassing and distancing do not encourage the production of valid information with which to formulate and develop a strategy, not to mention to implement it.

Consultant shortcomings in implementing productive reasoning

Edward de Bono (1969, 1972, 1982) provides a model for productive reasoning, which he calls lateral thinking. Lateral thinking can be used to find creative solutions to problems and encourage learning. De Bono also presents examples of human action that are counterproductive to learning. For example, human beings produce such patterns as 'We're right, you are wrong.' These and other behavioral examples de Bono cites are similar to the Model I actions that produce Traps. Traps do not encourage human beings to seek new ways of thinking, to value discontinuity, and to seek to change the status quo.

I am suggesting that, in addition to the educational strategies that de Bono uses, it would be helpful to get the participants to focus on how they create Traps and how they deny that they are doing so, and deny that they are denying. I predict that as consultants learn lateral thinking they will compartmentalize it as a learning process to be used with clients who are 'smart' and who would enjoy lateral thinking. Under these conditions, the consultants are not likely to activate their fears about client pushback described earlier and again the Traps will become more robust.

Moore and Sonsino (2003), citing Toulmin, recommend that consultants craft arguments that are effective. This includes stating claims clearly, providing the grounds or data used to make claims and include qualifications, warrants, or backing for their claims. These requirements are consistent with productive reasoning embedded Model II inquiry and testing.

Moore and Sonsino recommend using the Toulmin model in order to bring the clients 'into your way of thinking' (2003: 26). They continue that sound argumentation will lead to a greater sense of confidence on the part of the consultants, and make it more likely that they will feel less vulnerable. This, the authors claim, should assist the actors to persuade others more effectively. These quotations indicate that the consultants are advised to be in unilateral control and to parry clients' queries. Not surprisingly, the authors recommend that the consultants should implement the above before they 'go public' because the clients would be less likely to experience their arguments as being based on personal opinion or that they are crafted to be imposed. The advice is consistent with Model I values of unilateral control and cover-up of the unilateral control.

The authors also advise that the Toulmin model should be used to produce arguments that are more likely to be seen as truthful. Yet they should do so in private, in case the clients disagree and attack. On the one hand, the consultants should use a model for seeking truth by all parties that encourages symmetry of powers in the relationship. On the other hand, if it is necessary to defend their argument they should cover themselves in ways that create asymmetrical power and act as if they are not covering themselves. To the extent that the clients use Model I and defensive reasoning, they will create asymmetrical relationships. All this is not discussable and its undiscussability is undiscussable.

To review, those who seek real change in organizations should not expect outside consultants to be able to create miracles. As human beings, consultants are not immune to responding to situations that are threatening or embarrassing with Model I theory-in-use and defensive reasoning. Real change must often come from within.

The Collaborative Community

A number of professionals who work in organization development and leadership seek to model the workings of organizations on the more organic workings of natural communities. A central theme in *The Firm as a Collaborative Community: Reconstructing Trust in the Knowledge Economy* by Heckscher and Adler (2006) is that a central tension has run through social analysis for well over a century. The issue of community and trust seem increasingly necessary in a complex interdependent world but they are increasingly less available. Bonds of trust are essential yet they are eroding when they are most needed.

Heckscher and Adler describe three forms of community. The first is hierarchical, and market oriented. The second is community as the dominant principle. The third community, the collaborative community, is necessary if trust is to be reconstructed in the modern world. The values of a collaborative community are contribution, concern, honesty, congeniality. There is an emphasis on high collectivism and individualism as well as high particularism and universalism. The collaborative community, they believe, will flourish with minimal Traps and high trust.

A collaborative community requires different expectations than hierarchical and market communities. Movement toward the collaborative community will cause the established webs of traditional mutual expectations to tear. The overall level of trust will decline and people will withdraw into self-protective individualism.

The authors claim that in order for collaborative communities to flourish it is necessary to change the norms of deference, of autonomy (do not invade others' turf), and of stovepipe structures. They also point out that some common features of Traps need to be reduced or eliminated: the designed strategy of being respectful in public while privately maintaining that the others are not worthy of respect and the tendency of people to take refuge in the belief that they are victims of their organizations and that they are helpless to make appropriate changes.

The authors are clear that moving from here to there will not be easy. They review the attempts made to create collaborative communities and conclude that success to date is mixed. They select an intervention process created by Beer and his colleagues (1997) as one that has potential in moving us from here to there.

The Strategic Fitness Process

The Strategic Fitness Process (SFP) is a process of building a collaborative community. It is based on building a learning process that encourages inquiry into all aspects and at all levels, especially at the top. Inquiry is coupled with advocacy and testing of ideas—features of Model II theory-in-use and productive reasoning.

For example, the top management of a large corporation asked, 'What are the strengths of the organizations and what barriers do we see to implementing the strategy?' A task force was appointed composed of managers who had a reputation for being honest and showing little respect for deference. They were provided with a course in interviewing. They then interviewed many individuals, at all levels, throughout the organization. Next, with the help of professionals, they made their analysis. They identified the following six barriers to be overcome if success was to be achieved. First, strategy was unclear and represented conflicting priorities. The employees had not heard the strategy articulated previously; it did not make sense to them and various components were inconsistent with each other. Second, there was an ineffective top team. The employees perceived lack of cooperation and agreement at the top. Too many meetings at the top were filled with administrative rather than strategic issues. Third, there was a top–down or laissez-faire leadership style by the general manager. Fourth, there was poor coordination and teamwork across key interfaces. Fifth, there was poor vertical communication. Sixth, management and leadership skills were inadequate throughout the organization.

The findings were discussed by the top management and members of the task force. The former then met privately to develop corrective actions such as (a) develop the top team to deal more effectively with conflicts and to develop better unity in strategic direction; (b) inform lower levels with one voice of the direction in which the organization should go; (c) learn from lower levels about organizational arrangements and their own top team behavior that blocked effective implementation and reformulation of organizational strategies. Those involved, especially top management, evaluated the program as very effective. One senior executive said that this intervention made it possible for the top to discuss the undiscussables. Once they reached agreement, they formulated policies and practices to reduce the undiscussables around the strategy.

The structure of the process made it possible to achieve this progress. For example, the top management publicly committed themselves to detect errors, such as the barriers, and to correct them. The task force members could bypass the counterproductive forces of Traps by holding the top responsible that tough analysis would not be career threatening. This led the task force to accept personal responsibility for producing a valid albeit tough analysis. Finally, the focus of the report included undiscussables in the above ground organization that could be changed.

Let us dig a bit deeper. The respondents who were interviewed knew about the six barriers. They were able to provide evidence for their existence. So why did the organization not take action earlier? What were the obstacles to making the barriers transparent and actionable? What does this inaction say about leadership and about the organizational culture?

Also, if the middle managers knew about the barriers, what prevented them from pushing for action long before the intervention helped to legitimize their becoming more candid? What actions, if any, did the top and the middle managers take to cover up what they knew and to cover up that they were covering up?

One might ask what difference all this makes. After all, the problems were identified and made discussable, an achievement not to be belittled. The answer depends on the meaning of the word 'problems'. If 'problems' means the barriers to effectiveness were identified by the task force then progress was made. If, in addition, 'problems' means also the obstacles created, for many months, by the participants that prevented the detection and correction of the six barriers, then this problem has not been solved. The Traps that created the barriers still exist, in the underground world, waiting for the next problems to be solved. Thus the first-order problems may have been solved but, at best, the solution will be limited to the strategy issues. The second-order problems have not been solved, hence the changes are not likely to persevere.

Heckscher (2007) expands his views on how to move away from the old approach of unilateral leadership and control in the service of loyalty to the new approach of the flexible collaborative enterprise. Again, he suggests that the Strategic Fitness Process created by Michael Beer and his colleagues be used to provide paths to effective change. Recall the process for change is itself collaborative. 'The task team tells the top managers that their ideas of what is happening in the organization do not reflect reality' (Heckscher 2007: 230). The reports are described as being candid, blunt, tough, and at times brutal. The descriptions are consistent with Model I theory-in-use. The middle level reporters advocate their views and they make evaluations and attributions in ways that do not encourage the top to question their findings. Heckscher reports that these first feedback sessions shake the top. He reports that the top develops feelings of anger, hurt, and denial. 'It's not surprising that in almost every case there are members of top leadership who retreat to various forms of resistance' (2007: 231). Defensive reasoning appears to be activated in addition to Model I theory-in-use.

Heckscher continues that the middle-level team and the senior leadership find this 'opening up' so novel that no one feels able to predict where it will go. The lower levels wonder about the dangers they are running in speaking honestly with their superiors. The superiors worry about losing control. They fret that they could handle the change by just telling people what to do. These consequences are consistent with the Traps.

The process is designed to minimize counterproductive consequences by having rules that permit the reporters to be candid and state that the top managers must listen in silence. They can only speak to clarify and to test their understanding. The top managers will be able to express their feelings and reactions when they meet privately with each other. This rule legitimizes any catharsis that the top seeks to express. It also legitimizes a distancing between the top and the middle. The distancing prevents the self-fueling, counterproductive consequences that would result from the suppressed left-hand column of the top and the Traps processes that they would be activating if the distancing did not occur. The consultants flag behaviors on anyone's part that would activate Traps.

There is a problem involved with these positive results. They prevent counterproductive actions by distancing the participants from each other. They also 'teach' a strategy of leadership that encourages distancing. The Traps are bypassed. They are not confronted. This danger can be dealt with by the consultants discussing it with the participants. If the participants wish to reduce it, they could undergo learning to reduce Traps.

There are cases on record where the top management has not chosen to undergo such education. However, they have employed the Strategic Fitness Process in resolving other problems using whatever local designs that they found appropriate. Thus the organization has available to it a way of dealing with important problems yet not having to focus directly on reducing the Traps that remain underground.

Two observations are appropriate here. First, solving difficult problems is not a trivial success, especially when the managers acknowledge the limits of the process that they chose. Second, as the SFP is used, it may lead individuals to begin to move to learn the double-loop process of reducing Traps. This may lead to incremental movement toward a greater sense of community and collaboration. It may also provide opportunities for learning the skills necessary to reduce Traps, although there is as yet no evidence available to indicate what happens if SFP and the theory of action described in this book are combined. Such experiments may strengthen the use of 'communities of practice' in networking and organizational learning for effective problem-solving. Perhaps the most important consequences of including an approach that reduces Traps is that it may reduce the likelihood that change programs will be experienced as false and dishonest, a consequence that Heckscher notes occurs more frequently than it should.

Cooperation without trust

As opposed to Heckscher and Adler, who argue that bonds of trust are essential in a complex, interdependent world, Cook, Hardin, and Levi (2005) argue in *Cooperation Without Trust?* that a society can function well in the absence of trust. These authors suggest that, although interpersonal trust is important, especially in face to face situations, such trust is inadequate to design and lead organizations. I suggest that their theory of trust, if implemented, contains contradictions that limit its validity and its generalizability. I also suggest possible strategies to overcome the limits.

The authors define trust as follows: 'Trust exists when one party of the relationship believes the other party has the incentive to act in his or her interest or to take his or her interests to heart' (Cook *et al.* 2005: 2). Trust entails the claim, 'For us to trust you requires both that we suppose you are competent to perform what we trust you to do and that we suppose your reasoning for doing so is not merely your immediate interest but also your concern with our interest and well being' (ibid. 7).

Embedded in these definitions is a causal theory about the conditions that are necessary to implement trust. The claim may be briefly stated as follows. If the first party has the incentive and the competence to act in the other's interest, and if the first party genuinely believes it is in his interest to do so, and if there are no 'externalities' to prevent the first party from acting consistently with what she or he intends, then he or she will do so.

The existence of Traps prevents the causal theory from being as seamless as intended because Model I theory-in-use and defensive reasoning are 'internal' to every actor. Thus actors choose to deal with the 'externalities' by a theory-in-use and defensive reasoning for which the actor is responsible. For example, Rusk believed that it was in his best interest and the interests of the Foreign Service for it to become more effective, and in the interest of the State Department for it to lose its reputation of 'Foggy Bottom'.

173

Rusk also knew that the reputation of 'Foggy Bottom' had a long history. State officials before him and those then in active service had acted to create and maintain that reputation. They also covered up their personal responsibility for doing so. Moreover, they covered up the cover-up by making these actions undiscussable. To close the loop they created norms to sanction these actions, which protected them from being held personally responsible for the counterproductive consequences that became transparent.

Rusk's officials trusted Rusk not to violate their interests. They understood Rusk's dilemma and predicted that he would act in ways to espouse change while his theory-in-use would be to champion such changes in ways that gave himself and his associates room to protect themselves by using the Traps. The reader may recall that he acted consistently with their predictions. All of these actions are consistent with Cook's, Hardin's, and Levi's concept of trust as encapsulated interest. All parties had an important incentive to be trustworthy and this incentive is grounded in the value of maintaining future relationships of trust. Thus all parties involved rightly trusted each other to maintain the Trap of 'Foggy Bottom'.

These comments lead me to ask, what does the theory predict about the consequences when individuals believe they are acting consistently with being trustworthy, yet they know that they are spinning and acting as if they are not? What is the impact on individuals who learn that cooperation can come to mean that individuals may have powerful negative left-hand columns and act as if they do not? What is the impact of individuals when they lead a life of denials and denials of the denials?

How would the authors' theory of encapsulated trust explain this behavior? Does the theory help them to design social experiments in order to reduce the anti-learning self-sealing activities? Would not such experiments, whatever their results, enlarge and define their theory?

The authors claim the interpersonal trust can help to lower costs of monitoring and sanctioning that might be required by individuals who were not trustworthy. But the interpersonal Model I trust and the Traps may actually increase the costs of monitoring and sanctioning. Moreover they may drive the dysfunctional consequence underground, making it even more likely that the potential tragedies will not be discovered until a tragedy occurs that is public and dramatic.

Structural Approaches

Addressing organizational structure is another way management researchers propose to overcome the typical problems of organizations. The focus is not so much on people and their behavior as on the organizational rules—structures—that bind them together. While there are many structural approaches to revamping organizations, ranging from flattening to re-engineering, we will examine two such suggestions here, involving X-teams and ambi-dextrous organizations.

X-teams

Ancona and Bresman suggest that effective performance requires the development of X-teams. X-teams balance internal and external competencies. The authors claim that an overemphasis has been placed on the internal factors. Not enough emphasis has been placed on 'the years of research and practice . . . that has shown that managing externally enables teams to lead, innovate, and succeed in a rapidly changing environment' (2007: 6). X-teams engage in high levels of scouting, ambassador-ship, and task coordination.

Ancona and Bresman also recognize that, although groups become more effective in their external relationships, they will still need to develop their competence in dealing with each other. For example, with more information, complicated trade-offs arise and the decisions are more difficult to make. 'When divergent political interests enter the team, those external can become internal team conflicts' and 'Extreme execution inside the team becomes more important' (2007: 91).

Examples of 'upgrading' includes going beyond traditional boundaries, expanding the involvement by the development of expandable tiers, and exchangeable membership. If these characteristics are implemented correctly the teams will become more innovative. Their interactions with others will be more effective and the teams are more likely to produce a more effective product. The reasoning is, if teams upgrade, they will get in more relevant information, become more agile, and more innovative. Therefore teams with these characteristics will outperform traditional teams.

The authors introduce a proviso. X-teams are *not* needed when (1) team goals are not needed, (2) organizational goals are clearly aligned, (3) the team has the support it needs, (4) when they have all the information that they require, (5) when the knowledge required is not changing rapidly, and (6) when the team's task is not highly interdependent with others within the organization.

However, the authors make it clear that their advice on X-teams may meet resistance. For example, 'of course not all conversations are successful. Sometimes management simply does not want to listen to new ideas or thinks that such ideas are not a priority' (Ancona and Bresman 2007: 79). The authors' advice to deal with these problems is to continue the lobbying effort or move on to something else and presumably act as if they are not rejecting management. They then add that this is where being X-team members requires courage and determination. However they do not specify how people can acquire these qualities.

The authors realize that organizations are political entities. People hoard resources and hold grudges. They guard their turf and strike at those who try to take it away. The authors advise X-team members to find people with power and influence who are willing to protect the team. Again, the authors do not specify the theory-in-use that they believe is required if the advice is to be implemented effectively. If the advice is, in effect, to be realistic and to realize that transparency could be harmful then the actions that follow would be consistent with cover-up and covering up the cover-ups. All these consequences are consistent with a victim mentality that is a foundation of Traps. Would it not help the potential users of the advice to be clear about the possible Trap costs of their actions to the long-term health of their organization?

The authors also advise that effective exploration is implemented by the participants suspending prior views, looking at the world with new eyes, finding hidden opportunities, and creating open dialogue. In order for this advice to be implemented, the participants must have the requisite skills and reasoning processes, such as Model II theories-in-use and productive reasoning. As we have shown, when Traps are active, it is unlikely that the participants will have the skills and the productive reasoning processes, or if they do it is unlikely that they will use them.

The authors advise the participants to produce buy in, to lobby, to crusade, to protect the team from political adversaries by cajoling and 'friendly' coercion. If the advice is implemented by using Model I theory-in-use and defensive reasoning, then it will result in cover-up and covering up the cover-up. This will then result in mixed messages. For example: see the world in new ways but be careful. Use distributed leadership but be unilaterally strong. Be a champion of change but be realistic. Create cultural change programs but create them in ways that they are not trusted.

In closing, the authors express doubt about the effectiveness of current human relations change programs because they are too oriented internally. Their doubts are valid. For example, many senior OD consultants and change professional begin with the premise that their clients must feel genuine pain if they are to change. When the clients respond that their pain is about solving business and organizational issues, the consultants interpret such a response as being too rational and thereby denying their pain. Often they guide their inquiry to examine the personal pain even though the clients question the validity of their diagnosis. Transcripts from actual sessions with such professionals show that their premise that the clients must feel pain may be an act of defensive reasoning. The consultants begin with this premise because it fits with their psychological-clinical skills and it covers up their inability to think and act beyond them. (Argyris 2000, 2004).

The Ambidextrous Organization

Today's organizations need to deal with continuity and change—a challenge that pulls the organization in two different directions. In *Winning through Innovation: A Practical Guide to Leading Organizational Change and Renewal*, Tushman and O'Reilly III (2002) claim that successful managers are faced with a paradox. In order to compete in mature markets, they create structures, processes, and systems that lead to success. This produces a mind-set of uniformity and conformity. People become committed to the status quo. They become arrogant, reinforced by their previous success. *There is a turn inward*. This reduces their flexibility to deal with emergent markets. This results in the paradox that the authors label 'the tyranny of success'. Success in a stable environment enhances the chances of failure when the environment shifts.

The tyranny of today's success can be overcome by creating ambidextrous organizations: organizations with internally inconsistent competencies, structures, and cultures yet with a single vision. The authors state that it is not easy to create ambidextrous organizations. They also provide a learning framework by which they can be created. Step 1 is to identify the manager and the unit of analysis and performance or opportunity gaps. Step 2 is to describe critical task and work processes. Step 3 is to check for organizational consequences between task-formal organization, task-people, task, and culture. Step 4 is to develop solutions and take actions. Step 5 is to observe responses and learn from consequences. The authors provide detailed descriptions to implement these steps.

If my understanding is correct, they do not include the challenge of dealing with Traps. They may believe that Traps are not likely to arise in creating ambidextrous organizations. It is difficult to accept this explanation since these organizations require a high degree of mutual respect, openness, trust, collaboration, teamwork, and risk-taking. However, both claims are subject to test.

The authors cite the example of the CEO of Grenzack who asked his top group to prepare an obituary describing how and when they believed Grenzack would fail and die. All the managers predicted that if the present conditions were left unchanged, the organization would fail within the next several years. One common cause of death was identified as 'a lack of agreement and focus among management about problems' (Tushman and O'Reilly: 2002: 61).

The team listed five problems and presented detailed proposals as to how to solve them. The observation made above regarding the Strategic Fitness Process applies here as well: while reaching agreement on the five critical problems is not a trivial achievement, neither the CEO nor the team considered the question of how long had they known about these problems. How long did they have ideas about how to solve them? What prevented them from taking appropriate actions earlier?

Engaging in dialogue over these questions would uncover if any Traps existed. What would happen if the managers developed ambidextrous mind-sets that combined dealing with the above ground task world and the Traps? So far the successful interventions described do not touch the Traps. They still exist in the underground organizations. Would it not have been an important lesson for the managers and the organizations to examine these issues?

For example, the authors recommend that, in order for their framework to be effective people must be motivated to change: 'The first and most important step in motivating constructive behavior is to ensure that people understand emotionally, not just intellectually, why they have to change' (ibid. 199). To accomplish this they advise that a credible crisis be created. Such a crisis would provide energy to promote motivation and engagement. But an observer may ask, if the Grenzack CEO and his executives were able to identify five causes of death, why do they need an enemy to motivate them to change? Why not include upfront the possibility that they too are their own enemies?

What are the likely results of the CEO using a 'doom speech' to motivate change? If Traps are operating, will not a 'doom speech' make it easier for Traps to flourish because such speeches can encourage in the managers the Trap mentality that they believe they are not personally responsible for the crisis, because they are victims. Often such speeches are followed with specific advice to the organization as to how to overcome the problems. Managers may appreciate the advice because they can use it to confirm that they are victims and (without the top) they are helpless.

Human Potential

Many approaches to strengthening organizational per-formance focus on the characteristics of the human actors who make up organizations, based on the belief that humans have a far greater potential for achievement than they are able to tap into. These approaches range from those that focus on psychological qualities to those that suggest ways to enhance learning. They could also become more robust by addressing existence of Traps, as we shall see.

Psychological capital

And now we come to an approach that looks directly at the psychology of the individuals who make up organizations. In *Psychological Capital: Developing the Human Competitive Edge*, Luthans, Yousseff, and Avolio (2007) present a new model of how competitive advantage can be increased by increasing a leader's or organization's degree of depth and psychological capital (PsyCap). PsyCap is composed of four capabilities. They are (1) efficacy: the individuals' conviction about their capability to execute a specific task successfully; (2) hope: individuals possess goal-directed willpower coupled with energy and determination; (3) optimism: individuals predict good things will happen in the future; and (4) resilience: individuals have the capacity to rebound from adversity, conflict, and failure.

The authors claim that if individuals score high on these four attributes the greater the likelihood that groups and organizations will also score high on these attributes. It is the synergistic effect of these attributes that increases the likelihood PsyCap will increase organizational effectiveness and competitive advantage. How can the research on Traps help to strengthen the likely success of PsyCap?

My first suggestion is to go beyond the instrument used to measure PsyCap, which only captures *espoused* theory, and include research which can assess theory-in-use and reasoning mind-set. As we have repeatedly seen, a person's espoused theory can be very different from his or her theory-in-use.

Recall that the thirty-four CEOs in Chapter 5 scored themselves high in efficacy to help Andy. That was their espoused theory when they began the case discussion. By focusing on their theory-in-use and their reasoning processes they learned that they were not competent to help Andy even under the conditions where Andy pleaded for help and the context was one of learning.

The CEOs did not believe that by the end of the seminar they would learn that they are skillful at producing Traps and skillfully blind that this is the case. Would it not help to enhance the value of PsyCap if it is possible to predict ahead of time that in order to deal effectively with Traps the individuals may have to experience unexpected failure which, in turn, may shake their faith in their sense of efficacy, hope, optimism, and resiliency about themselves and others? Pessimism may be a necessary experience to achieve realistic optimism.

Building on strengths

Including Traps may also help to set realistic expectations that managers have about building their own strengths and the strengths of others. For example Ross (2006) advises that individuals should begin their learning in areas where they have demonstrated competence. Perhaps she should also help the managers to realize how unlikely they are to be sound predictors of their competence.

Ross advises that managers should create a context where they can help each other improve. Ross would help the managers set more realistic levels of reachable goals if they are helped to see that the goals they are likely to set, in helping themselves and others, are not as easily reachable as they believe. Finally Ross advises that people should address failures factually. People should learn to accept more of their own personal responsibility for actions that they have taken and for the actual consequences that they produced.

Underlying the advice that Ross gives is that human beings can help each other to strengthen their PsyCap by striving to do so in a safe context. While there may be cases in which that is true, providing a safe context offers no guarantees, as demonstrated by the case of the CEOs and Andy.

Learning strategies

Dickmann and Stanford-Blair (2002: 91) connect leadership and the brain by stating that the human brain is 'a lean, mean, pattern-making machine'. Their causal reasoning is, *if* the brain is a lean, mean, pattern-making machine, *then* the leaders should forgo extensive efforts to instruct in favor of providing opportunities for individuals to construct personal knowledge. This is best implemented by educating leaders using a variety of venues—groups, conferences, and workshops where there are frequent opportunities for interactions.

We have a puzzle. Variety is recommended and personal involvement for whatever site that is chosen. Yet, if people come to these sites with Model I theory-in-use patterns and defensive reasoning, the site variety should make little or no difference at the theory-in-use level if Traps are involved. Dickmann and Stanford-Blair state that the human potential within the organization is its greatest asset. But it is also true that the same human beings may limit their potential by using Model I and defensive reasoning, and by depending on Traps to cover for them. 'Simply put, when one brain meets another brain, the exercise of intelligence in its multiple dimensions—inevitably follow' (ibid. 199). The dilemma is that part of the multiple dimensions of intelligence are knowledge and skills to prevent the learning being recommended by the author. How do we deal with this dilemma? The advice about multiple learning venues may be flawed because it bypasses the dilemmas described above.

Conclusion

We have examined a variety of approaches that are supposed to solve organizational problems and bring new levels of performance. They all have something of value to offer—yet they all also fall short in so far as they fail to address the existence of Traps. The crucial reality that many of these approaches overlook—no matter how innovative they seem on the surface—is that they must all be implemented by human beings, who although they often espouse Model II values and productive reasoning, usually retreat to the safety of Model I values and a defensive mind-set in action.

Conclusion

Traps and the Human Predicament

This book has been about how we get trapped by behavior that prevents learning and change—and that often works against our own best interests. We have examined why dysfunctional behavior is so prevalent in organizations and so hard to overcome. In broad strokes, we discovered that, when we most need to learn, we paradoxically work hardest at *shutting down* conversations, shutting down other people, and shutting down ourselves. We tell ourselves and each other, 'don't go there', where 'there' is any sensitive issue that might upset the status quo that envelops us like a cocoon. We have tacitly agreed to rule off limits, to make undiscussable, topics that challenge our accepted sense of self and our comfortable organizational routines. Having thus agreed to rule off limits any topics that might help us change and grow, we become trapped in the status quo. This is a problem that extends into every region of human endeavor—with far-reaching implications.

We started out examining two cases showing how very talented and accomplished men (Dean Rusk at the State Department and Andrew Grove at Intel) became tangled in Traps of their own making. Intelligent and experienced as they both were, they also were completely unaware of how their own behavior led to counterproductive results. They strove mightily to change their organizations and failed, even though they were at the top of the respective hierarchies.

We also saw that the Grove and Rusk cases are far from exceptional. In Chapter 2, we examined a wide variety of cases from ordinary people who described *in their own words* how they failed to achieve the results they intended. People tried to produce openness and transparency, increase learning, and improve cooperation (among other objectives), yet not one of these objectives was achieved. Puzzling as this behavior may seem on the surface, I suggested that almost every reader of this book recognized himself or herself in one or more of the cases.

We then examined the question of why human beings produce these sorts of results—results that are *counterproductive to their own stated interests and intentions*. The answer, we saw, is found in the fact that we all possess two theories of action, one of which we espouse, and one of which we actually use. These theories contain fundamental, systematic mismatches, making them inconsistent.

Research shows that almost everyone has Model I as their theory-in-use. As we saw, Model I reasoning represents our theory-in-use when we face threatening or potentially embarrassing situations. The objectives of this theory of action are: (1) be in unilateral control; (2) win and do not lose; (3) suppress negative feelings; and (4) behave rationally.

Model II, which many people espouse, but cannot use, has the following objectives: (1) seek valid (testable) information; (2) create informed choice; and (3) monitor vigilantly to detect and correct error. The purpose of Model I is to protect and defend the self against fundamental, disruptive change. As human beings become skillful in using Model I, they develop a defensive reasoning mind-set that they use to explain their actions and to design and implement future actions.

The purpose of Model II, on the other hand, is unrelated to the self: valid knowledge, which can be assessed and tested publicly. As individuals become skillful at using Model II, they will also become skillful at using productive reasoning. Productive reasoning can be used to make personal reasoning transparent in order for claims to be tested robustly. Model II governing values can lead to openness, transparency, and trust. However, empirical evidence shows that few people have a Model II theory-in-use.

The problem—and the reason we create Traps for ourselves—is that we espouse Model II reasoning when our actions are in fact based on Model I. Thus, we think we are acting in a way that creates trust, informed choice, and valid information, but in fact we are acting in ways that undermine those values in order to defend the self. We get trapped into avoiding discussions or learning that might disrupt the status quo. Traps create barriers not only for individuals, but also for groups, relations between groups, and entire organizations. How have researchers, consultants, and enlightened practitioners dealt with this?

The Attempt to Find New Ways Forward

With all the problems confronting modern organizations and modern societies—increased competition, increasingly rapid technological change, and burgeoning corruption to name a few—it is not surprising that we have witnessed an explosion of books and articles on improving organizational performance and effectiveness, on leading change, and on personal transformation. Many of these materials focus on leadership, organizational culture, and other approaches. Yet, as we reviewed these materials, we found that they have little to say about the problem of Traps.

We first focused on leadership and asked what advice would those seeking to reduce Traps get by reading the research on leadership written by some of our most celebrated and widely read researchers and experts. Is it useful? Is it implementable?

As we saw, readers of these books find little advice on how to reduce Traps that is implementable. Individuals seeking to act more effectively, especially to diagnose and reduce Traps, need to know their theory-in-use. They also need to know the degree to which they blame others and deny their personal causal responsibilities for creating Traps. They also need to know how Traps become self-fueling and self-sealing, with defensive reasoning obstructing the reduction of Traps. We reviewed the statistical and clinical literature on leadership. The data collected were primarily espoused theory data (question-naires and interviews). There was little attention paid to Model I theory-in-use and to defensive reasoning mind-set. The research on personality and narcissistic leaders recommended that, in order for leaders to be effective, they should act in ways that are consistent with Model I and defensive reasoning. No explicit attention was paid to the possibility that this would create Traps. Without attention paid to these factors (as well as Model II theory-in-use and productive reasoning) the advice derived from the research is not actionable in terms of reducing Traps.

We also argued that the works of the researchers reviewed in this book bypass the problem of reducing Traps because of the most fundamental assumptions they hold about effective research. In sum, the advice provided by these highly respected researchers is, at best, able to solve single-loop problems. The advice is inad-equate to diagnosing and reducing Traps.

Once we discovered that the literature on leadership wouldn't help us break through the Traps that envelop us, perhaps, we thought, organizational culture would be more successful. As we saw, culture is often presented as a miraculous cure for revitalizing organizations. But as we looked at the empirical evidence, using a classroom exercise in which thirty-four executives tried to help an executive named 'Andy' and an extensive case study of a culture change program at Shell, we did not find support for culture as a resource for reducing Traps. On the contrary, the evidence suggested that we must in fact address the Model I behavior that leads to Traps *before* we can change the culture.

We then looked at a variety of other approaches that have been presented as breakthroughs in solving organizational problems and increasing performance. These approaches focused on organizational performance through using outside consultants, improving the psychological well-being of its members, strengthening teamwork, promoting organizational learning, improving collaboration, ensuring strategic fit, and other strategies. A few of these new approaches addressed the existence of Traps in one form or another, but many seemed unaware of the existence of Traps, or simply bypassed them. As we saw, each approach can in fact be strengthened by including features of our approach in order to reduce Traps.

The proponents of appreciative inquiry did claim that their findings were actionable. They were; but for routine single-loop problems. In a case that the authors state represents a reduction of Traps, we found that their findings were consistent with Model I defensive reasoning.

The advice from PsyCap, ambidextrous organizations, and cooperation without trust did not include dealing with Traps, yet if their advice was implemented it could create Traps. For example, in the case of the ambidextrous organization, the authors advised leaders to motivate others by creating credible enemies and credible crises. They did not advise making this strategy transparent, perhaps because doing so would negate its effectiveness. In such cases the result is building a sense of mistrust because the subordinates often sensed the purpose of the strategy and why it had to be undiscussable.

The researchers on collaborative communities did provide examples of collaborative dialogue but it involved single-loop issues. In order to deal with double-loop problems they recommend the Strategic Fitness Process which indeed does differentiate between espoused theory and theory-in-use and does focus skills in productive reasoning. As we saw, this process works best when the clients are guided by the consultants as to how to make valid diagnosis and take action. The consultants created conditions where they are responsible for inducing clients to speak openly and with transparency in their reasoning. In short, the consultants are largely responsible for requiring the clients to violate defensive actions sanctioned by Traps.

The bottom line is that changes in top–down leadership structures, unilateral control systems, and reward policies can lead to small reductions of Traps. However they are unlikely to be effective and to persevere if Model II theories-in-use and productive reasoning do not become an integral part of the leadership, the culture, and organizational design. It is theories-in-use and reasoning processes that are primary.

In order to reduce Traps, we must begin by addressing Model I theories-in-use and defensive reasoning. Traps cannot be reduced by focusing on environmental factors such as new structures and reward policies. Individuals operating in such structures or under such policies will use the theory-in-use that they already hold and defensive reasoning to protect themselves.

To underscore the significance of the points made above, let me focus on a recent conference report.

Helping Moon Shots to Succeed

Much of the future progress on leadership culture and organizational design is inhibited by Traps. Practitioners are aware of these limits. Unfortunately they appear to bypass them. This is also true with scholars. Both groups appear to be unaware that the consequence of their respective bypass strengthens Traps. Let me give an example. As I was writing this book, I received a prepublication copy of a report that described a conference of about thirty-five executives, academics, consultants, entrepreneurs, and venture capitalists who were selected to attend a conference whose objective was to make management practice and theory more meaningful for the twenty-first century. The challenge was: 'No less momentous than the ones that gave birth to the Industrial Age' (Hamel 2009: 92).

The report describes twenty-five critical innovative practices that are called 'moon shots'. I have selected six that were described as more critical to provide the reader with an idea of the kinds of recommendations made in the report.

1. Ensure that management's work serves a higher purpose that goes beyond maximizing shareholders' wealth.

2. Create collaborative systems that will outperform those characterized by adversarial, win–lose relationships. These systems must reflect the ethos of community and citizenship.

3. Reconstruct management's philosophical foundations that are not only operationally excellent; they must also be adaptable, innovative, inspiring, and socially responsible.

4. Eliminate the pathologies associated with formal hierarchy such as top–down authority structures that provide followers with little or no influence in choosing their leaders, that perpetuate power disparities, and that undermine the self-worth of those who have little formal power.

5. Increase trust and reduce mistrust so that risk-taking is encouraged and contentious opinions freely expressed.

6. Increase the numbers of individuals who are capable of self-responsibility.

There is a puzzle embedded in the list of 'moon shots'. On the one hand, the list makes good sense. Implementing these recommendations successfully would go a long way to achieving the objectives of the conference. On the other hand, I suggest that the moon shots the conference-goers came up with are not news to many practitioners and researchers who attend university or company executive programs or those who keep up to date with the current literature as described in this book. Knowledgeable people have been calling for these reforms and others for at least three decades. Yet here we have these recommendations from a recent conference of prestigious executives, consultants, venture capitalists—presented as if many of their peers had not been working assiduously on achieving these results for years. How can this be?

Why did the conference organizers not direct the energy and attention of researchers and executives to begin to *change the status quo* so that these moon shots could be achieved? One reason why the participants at this prestigious conference could present these recommended moon shots with such unselfconsciousness could be our collective decision to treat our inability to actually achieve these results as undiscussable. We have collectively decided to rule discussion of the power and ubiquity of Traps off limits. It may be unfair to call them naïve, yet we must point out that those who overlook the power and ubiquity of Traps will find their prescriptions for change continuously undermined.

The Human Predicament

We must now ask some hard questions. Given all the advice from literally hundreds of books and thousands of articles that have appeared over the past decades (of which we have examined but a small sample), have we witnessed a flowering of new forms of human potential? Have we been astounded by new levels of organizational performance and creativity? Is the world healing through international learning and cooperation? Anyone familiar with recent history knows the disappointing, even sad, answers to these questions. The world continues apace and we make incremental technological improvements here and there—but on the big questions we move not an inch. We are stuck. In fact, we are trapped.

I should like to focus upon the barriers that making Traps undiscussable has on our ability to deal with serious human problems. Ruling the discussion of Traps off limits makes learning in any deep sense about ourselves, our organizations, and our society almost impossible—and so protects the status quo even when we all recognize that change is needed and urgent. A great deal of the theory and practice of organizational research over the past few decades has been unable to change this situation.

Traps are thus a major problem confronting us today—as we face challenges on scales rarely witnessed in history: global warming, genocide, economic meltdown, political instability, and more. And as our problems grow, our capacity to deal with them seems to diminish. For example, Anand, Ashforth, and Joshi (2005) describe increasing fraud and corruption in modern societies. Frankel (2005) claims that wrongness, dishonesty, and mistrust are increasingly being normalized. Zak (2008) and her contributors suggest moral growth, sympathy, and human rights are being systematically downplayed. Posner (2009) provides insights into how defensive reasoning and actions distorting the making of judicial laws facilitated the failure of capitalism. On a rare positive note, Rappert (2007) indicates how attention to our perspective may help to influence research in biotechnology and search for security and limits. Sunstein (2009) claims that cultural polarization is becoming increasingly personal and political. Finally, Shane (2009) states that the executive power is used in ways that threaten American democracy because of unwillingness to confront key assumptions and profound disagreements, peer pressure to sidestep controversial decisions, and hostility to dissent. All these are key features of Traps.

As we noted in Chapter 4, researchers and consultants, as much as practicing managers, are prone to fall into Traps. As with all humans, they are protecting their sense of self and self-worth—and react quickly and without thinking to threats against the same—defensive behavior that is intended to shut down or divert uncomfortable discussions of the truth. Although the advice we have examined is created by a diverse group of researchers and thoughtful practitioners, they have one feature in common: namely that, for most of them, the distinction between espoused theory and theory-in-use is not a central component of their theory of intervention. They do not deny that this distinction is relevant. They choose not to focus their work upon it. In short, they do not discuss it.

One consequence is that they do not strive to diagnose their equivalent to Model I and Model II theory-in-use as well as defensive reasoning. As we have seen, most of their advice is ineffective or even beside the point when it skirts the problem of reducing Traps. In a few cases, I have shown that their advice actually strengthens Traps.

In closing, Traps are patterns created to prevent embarrassment or threat when the intention is to produce more effective action. Traps contain a fundamental dilemma. When we use them to design and produce effective action, and we do so correctly, they result primarily in counterproductive consequences. It is not possible to have just the productive consequences.

There are those who believe that aspiring to reduce Traps is naïve and impractical. They may be correct, but I doubt it. Changing will not be easy but I suggest that we have no other choice. We have seen the corrosive impact of Traps in organizations. We have seen that the new improvements that information science provides for more effective action are accompanied by a concomitant growth of Traps that are hidden in the underground organization. Traps are spreading and are becoming more powerful regardless of the methods that we use to try to reduce them. These methods do not reduce Traps; they bypass them. I have tried to suggest in this book that bypassing Traps is a moral hazard of the highest magnitude.

Bibliography

Anand, V., Ashforth, B. E., and Joshi, M. (2005) 'Business as Usual: The Acceptance and Perpetuation of Corruption in Organizations', *Academy of Management Executive*, 1a/4: 9–23.

Ancona, D., and Bresman, H. (2007) *X-Teams: How to Build Teams that Lead, Innovate and Succeed* (Boston: Harvard Business School Press).

Argyris, C. (1967) 'On the Future of Laboratory Education', *Journal of Applied Behavioral Science*, 3: 153–83.

—— (1968a) 'Conditions for Competence Acquisition and Therapy', *Journal of Applied Behavioral Science*, 4: 147–77.

—— (1968b) Some Causes of Organizational Ineffectiveness within the Department of State (Washington, D.C.: Center for International Systems Research, Occasional Papers, 2).

—— (1980) *Inner Contradictions of Rigorous Research* (San Diego, Calif.: Academic Press).

—— (1982) *Reasoning, Learning and Action: Individual and Organizational* (San Francisco: Jossey-Bass).

—— (1985) *Strategy, Change and Defensive Routines* (New York: Harper Business).

—— (1990a) *Overcoming Organizational Defenses* (Needham, Mass.: Allyn Bacon).

—— (1993) *Knowledge for Action: A Guide for Overcoming Barriers to Organizational Change* (San Francisco: Jossey-Bass).

Bibliography

Argyris, C. (1999) *On Organizational Learning* (2nd edn. Oxford: Blackwell Publishers).

—— (2000) *Flawed Advice and the Management Trap: How Managers can Know When they are Getting Good Advice and When they're Not* (New York: Oxford University Press).

—— (2002) 'Double-Loop Learning, Teaching, and Research', *Academy of Management Learning and Education*, 1: 206–19.

—— (2004) *Reasons and Rationalization: The Limits to Organizational Knowledge* (New York: Oxford University Press).

—— (2005) 'On the Demise of Organizational Development', in D. L. Bradford and W. W. Burke (eds.), *Reinventing Organizational Development* (San Francisco: Pfeffer Press), 113–30.

—— and Schön, D. (1996) *Organizational Learning*, ii. *Theory, Method and Practice* (Reading, Mass.: Addison-Wesley).

—— Putnam, R., and Smith, D. (1985) *Action Science* (San Francisco: Jossey-Bass).

Avolio, B. J. (2007) 'Promoting More Integrative Strategies for Leadership Theory-Building', *American Psychologist*, 63/1: 25–33.

—— and Bass, B. M. (2004) *Multifactor Leadership Questionnaires* (Lincoln, Neb.: Mind Garden, Inc.).

Barrett, F., and Cooperrider, D. L. (2007) 'Generative Metaphor Intervention: A New Approach for Working with Systems Divided by Conflict and Caught in Defensive Perception', *Journal of Applied Behavioral Science*, 26/2: 219–39.

—— Seiling, J., and Cooperrider, D. (2002) *Appreciative Inquiry, Organizational Transformation* (Westport, Conn.: Quorum), 39–66.

Bass, B. M., and Avolio, B. J. (1995) 'Multifactor Leadership Questionnaire', *Leaders Handbook* (Lincoln, Neb.: Mind Garden, Inc.).

—— and Riggio, R. E. (2006) *Transformational Leadership* (Mahwah, N.J.: Lawrence Erlbaum Associates).

Beer, M. (1997) *Leading Learning and Learning to Lead: An Action Approach to Developing Organizational Fitness* (Harvard Business School Working Paper Series, 98-035).

Bennis, W. (2003) *On Becoming a Leader* (rev. edn. New York: Basic Books).

—— and Thomas, R. J. (2002) *Geeks and Geezers* (Boston: Harvard Business School Press).

———— (2007) *Leading for a Lifetime* (Boston: Harvard Business School Press).

Boonstra, J. J., and de Caluwe, L. (2007) *Intervening and Changing Looking for Meaning in Interactions* (London: John Wiley & Sons Ltd).

Bower, J. (2007) *The CEO Within: Why Inside Outsiders are the Key to Succession Planning* (Cambridge, Mass.: Harvard Business School Press).

Brown, R. (1966) *New Direction in Psychology* (New York: Holt, Rinehart, & Winston).

Burns, T., and Stalker, G. M. (1961) *The Management of Innovation* (London: Tavistock).

Bushe, G. (2001) ' "Meaning Making in Teams": Appreciative Inquiry with Pre Identity and Post Identity in Groups', in R. Fry, F. Barrett, J. Seiling, and D. Whitney (eds.), *Appreciative Inquiry and Organizational Transformation: Reports from the Field* (Westport, Conn.: Quorum), 39–63.

Clark, S., and Myers, M. (2007) *Managing Difficult Conversations* (Cheltenham: Management Books).

Cook, K. S., Hardin, R., and Levi, M. (2005) *Cooperation Without Trust?* (New York: Russell Sage Foundation).

Cooperrider, D. L., and Srivastva, S. (2002) *Appreciative Inquiry, Organizational Transformation* (Westport, Conn.: Quorum), 39–66.

———— and Whitney, D. (2005) *Appreciative Inquiry* (San Francisco: Barrett-Koehler).

Dalton, M. A., and Ernst, C. T. (1998) 'Developing Leaders for Global Roles', in C. D. McCauley, R. S. Moxley, and E. Van Velsor (eds.), *The Center for Creative Leadership Handbook of Leadership Development* (San Francisco: Jossey-Bass), 361–82.

de Bono, E. L. (1969) *The Mechanism of Mind* (New York: Simon & Schuster).

———— (1972) *Lateral Thinking for Management* (New York: American Management Association).

———— (1982) *de Bono's Thinking Course* (New York: Facts on File Publication).

Dickmann, M. H., and Stanford-Blair, N. (2002) *Connecting Leadership to the Brain* (Thousand Oaks, Calif.: Corwin Press).

Frankel, T. (2005) *Trust and Honesty* (Oxford: Oxford University Press).

Frey, R., Barrett F., Seiling, J., and Whitney. D. (2001) *Appreciative Inquiry and Organizational Transformation: Reports from the Field* (Westport, Conn.: Quorum Books).

Bibliography

Gerzon, M. (2006) *Leading through Conflict* (Boston: Harvard Business School Press).

Grant, S., and Humphries, M. (2007) 'Critical Evaluation of Appreciative Inquiry: Bridging and Apparent Paradox', *Action Research*, 4: 401–18.

Grove, Andrew S. (1996) *Only the Paranoid Survive* (New York: Doubleday).

Hamel, G. (2009) 'Moon Shots for Management', *Harvard Business Review* (Feb., Reprint R0902H): 91–8.

Heckscher, C. C. (2007) *The Collaborative Enterprise: Managing Speed and Complexity in Knowledge-Based Business* (New Haven: Yale University Press).

—— and Adler, P. (2006) *The Firm as a Collaborative Community: Reconstructing Trust in the Knowledge Economy* (Oxford: Oxford University Press), 479–512.

—— and Foote, N. (2007) *The Collaborative Enterprise* (New Haven: Yale University Press).

Kegan, R., and Lahey, L. L. (2001) *How the Way We Talk Can Change the Way We Work* (San Francisco: Jossey-Bass Wiley).

—— —— (2001) 'The Real Reason People Won't Change', *Harvard Business Review* (Nov.): 85–92.

—— —— (2009) *Immunity to Change* (Cambridge, Mass.: Harvard University Press).

Lafley, A. G., and Charan, R. (2008) *The Game Changer* (New York: Crown Business).

Linden, J. D. (2007) *The Accidental Mind* (Cambridge, Mass.: Harvard University Press).

Lipchitz, R., Freedman, V. J., and Popper, M. (2007) *Demystifying Organizational Learning* (London: Sage).

Losey, M., Messinger, S., and Ulrich, D. (2006) *The Future of Human Resource Management* (New York: John Wiley).

Luthans, F., Yousseff, C. M., and Avolio, B. J. (2007) *Psychological Capital* (Oxford: Oxford University Press).

Macoby, M. (2007) *The Leaders We Need: And What Makes us Follow* (Cambridge, Mass.: Harvard Business School Press).

Manzoni, J. F., and Barsoux, J. L. (2002) *The Set-Up-To-Fail Syndrome* (Boston: Harvard Business School Press).

Martin, R. (2007) *The Opposable Mind: How Successful Leaders Win through Integrative Thinking* (Boston: Harvard Business School).

Mazen, A. M. (1997) 'Team Defensiveness: A Neglected Root Cause', *Administrative Science Quarterly*, 4/2: 24–50.

Moore, J., and Sonsino, S. (2003) *Leadership Unplugged: The New Renaissance of Value Propositions* (New York: Palgrave).

Mumford, M. D. (2006) *Pathways to Outstanding Leadership* (Mahwah, N.J.: Lawrence Erlbaum Associates).

Noonan, W. R. (2007) *Discussing the Undiscussable* (San Francisco: Jossey-Bass).

Posner, R. A. (2008) *How Judges Think* (Cambridge, Mass.: Harvard University Press).

Rappert, B. (2007) *Biotechnology, Security and the Search for Limits an Inquiry into Research and Methods* (London: Palgrave).

Romme, A., and Georges, L. (2003) 'Making a Difference: Organization as Design', *Organization Science*, 14/5: 558–73.

Ross, J. A. (2006) 'Making Every Leadership Moment Matter', *Harvard Management Update*, 3–5.

Rothschild, W. E. (2007) *The Secret to GE's Success* (New York: McGraw-Hill).

Runde, C. E., and Flanagan, T. A. (2007) *Becoming a Conflict Competent Leader: How You and Your Organization Can Manage Conflict Effectively* (San Francisco: John Wiley & Sons).

Sackman, S. A. (1991) *Cultural Knowledge in Organizations* (Newbury Park, Calif.: Sage).

Schein, E. H. (1992) *Organizational Culture and Leadership* (2nd edn. San Francisco: Jossey-Bass).

—— (1999) *The Corporate Culture Survival Guide* (San Francisco: Jossey-Bass).

—— (2002) *Organizational Culture and Leadership* (Md edn. San Francisco: Jossey-Bass).

Schmidt, C. (2005) 'Integration Theory and Practice in Industrial and Organizational Psychology Assessment: A Meta-Praxis Perspective', doctoral thesis, University of Johannesburg.

—— (2006) 'Validity as an Action Concept in I O Psychology', *SA Journal of Industrial Psychology*, 32/4: 59–67.

Schön, D. (1979) 'Generative Metaphor: A Perspective on Problem-Setting in Social Policy', in A. Ortony (ed.), *Metaphor and Thought* (Cambridge: Cambridge University Press), 137–63.

Schwarz, R. (2002) *The Skilled Facilitator* (San Francisco: Jossey-Bass).

Bibliography

Shane, P. M. (2009) *Madison's Nightmare: How Executive Power Threatens American Democracy* (Chicago: Chicago University Press).

Simon, H. A. (1969) *The Science of the Artificial* (Cambridge, Mass.: MIT Press).

Smith, D. M. (2008) *Divide or Conquer* (New York, Penguin).

Sunstein, C. R. (2009) *Going to Extremes: How Like Minds Unite and Divide* (Oxford: Oxford University Press).

Sutton, R. (2007) *The No Asshole Rule: Building an Analyzed Workplace and Surviving One That Isn't* (New York: Warner Business Book).

Tavris, C., and Aronson, E. (2007) *Mistakes Were Made (But Not By Me): Why We Justify Foolish Beliefs, Bad Decisions, and Hurtful Acts* (New York: Harcourt Books).

Taffinder, P. (2006) *The Leadership Crash Course* (London: Kogan Page).

Tichy, N., and Bennis, W. (2007) *Judgment: How Winning Leaders Make Great Allies* (New York: Penguin).

Turner, J. H. (2005) *The Sociology of Emotions* (Cambridge: Cambridge University Press).

Tushman, M. L., and O'Reilly III, C. A. (2002) *Winning through Innovation: A Practical Guide to Leading Organizational Change and Renewal* (Boston: Harvard Business School Press).

van Aken, J. E., Berends, H., and der van Bij, H. (2007) *Problem Solving in Organizations* (Cambridge: Cambridge University Press).

Want, J. (2006) *Corporate Culture* (New York: St Martin's Press).

Ward, K., Bowman, C., and Kakabadse, A. (2007) *Extraordinary Performance from Ordinary People* (Amsterdam: Elsevier).

WGBH (2007) *Athens Dawn of Democracy*, part 1 (Boston: Lion Television, aired 19 Nov.).

Wu, C., Neubert, M. J., and Yi, X. (2007) 'Transformational Leadership, Cohesion Perceptions, and Employee Cynicism about Organizational Change', *Journal of Applied Behavioral Science*, 43/3 (Sept.): 327–51.

Yukl, G. (2006) *Leadership in Organizations* (6th edn. Upper Saddle River, N.J.: Pearson, Prentice Hall).

Zaccaro, S. J. (2007) 'Fact-Based Perspective of Leadership', *American Psychologist*, 63: 6–16.

Zak, P. J., ed. (2008) *Moral Markets* (Princeton: Princeton University Press).

Index

Index

dialogue dominated by 28
distancing from 159
failure of capitalism facilitated
  by 198
internal to every actor 173
made transparent 112
pain and 179
prevalence of 70
reduction of Traps 89, 192
stronger 157
denial 78, 84, 112
  covering up 11, 147
  widespread 111
detail 19
Dickmann, M. H. 185, 186
difficult situations 11–24
dishonesty 131, 198
doom speeches 182
double-loop problems 194
dysfunctional behavior 1, 69, 175,
  188

education 19, 171
  leadership 126
efficacy 183, 184
emotional intelligence 96
emotions 155, 156, 182
EMT (Shell European Management
  Team) 126, 128, 134–5, 136,
  138, 142, 143, 148
enemies 182
enthusiasm 92
errors 122
  detection and correction of 2, 64,
    147, 168, 190
  learning from 123
  massive 57
  repeated 61
  responsibility for 61
espoused theory 61, 64, 67, 70, 91,
  141, 149, 150, 184
  advice given as abstract ideas
    based upon 86
  distinction between theory-in-use
    and 62, 85, 90, 104, 194, 199

inconsistencies between Model I
  theory-in-use and 89
variance in actual behavior
  of 74
evaluations and attributions 50, 51,
  53
executive power 199
expertise 95
externalities 173

failures 185, 198
feedback 119, 170
fight-or-flight responses 102
Financial Times 128
Flanagan, T. A. 102
France 127, 136
Frankel, T. 198
fraud 198

gasoline retail 127–8
Georges, L. 63 n.
Germany 136
Grant, S. 110 n.
Grenzack 181, 182
Grove, Andrew 5, 18, 19–22, 23, 58,
  60, 66, 75, 76, 86, 88, 91, 92, 93,
  94, 97, 101, 189
guilt 111

Hamel, G. 195
hard power 19
Hardin, R. 172, 173, 174
Heckscher, C. C. 165–6, 170, 172
hierarchical communities 165
honesty 2, 11, 13, 17, 23, 145, 166
  reputation for 167
hope 183, 184
hotels 108–10
human potential 182–6
Humphries, M. 110 n.

idealized influence 91
incentive plans 54
inconsistencies 19, 62, 79, 100,
  101, 111, 167

Index